BIBLE
UNDERSTANDING

Plus, others including
the "Circle of Love"

J. HARVEY HAMES

BIBLE UNDERSTANDING
PLUS, OTHERS INCLUDING THE "CIRCLE OF LOVE"

iUniverse books may be ordered through booksellers or by contacting:

iUniverse
1663 Liberty Drive
Bloomington, IN 47403
www.iuniverse.com
1-800-Authors (1-800-288-4677)

ISBN: 978-1-5320-8924-4 (sc)
ISBN: 978-1-5320-8925-1 (e)

Print information available on the last page.

iUniverse rev. date: 12/03/2019

"Things you have never heard or thought of before."

(This is my opinion. YOU CREATE YOUR OWN OPINION). Many things will be of a Spiritual world. JUST OPEN YOUR MIND TO NEW THINKING.

In this book you will read things you have NEVER thought of before. That does NOT mean they are NOT TRUE. OPEN YOUR MIND!

There are thousands of books in bookstores and libraries that you can read about the Bible. Many men and women have spent countless hours studying the Bible. In many of those books you can read a lot of details. This is not that type of book. In this book I wanted to tell you details you would NOT see in those other books. My goal is to get you to think about the Bible in a way you would WANT to study the Bible MORE.

This book is not written with large unknown words. It is written with simple everyday words easy to understand. There is no PHD after my name. I am just a simple person like most of the world. God changed my life at seven. When I became, older I went away from God. It was WRONG, and I am so sorry LORD. Before leaving this earth and go to Heaven, I just wanted to tell all of you what, I believe. Hope you enjoy reading what I have to say. If you do not believe everything, IT IS OKAY.

If you read something that does not keep your attention, please keep reading. Trust me, it WILL get better.

In the beginning of the Bible Moses wrote (Genesis 1:1). “In the beginning God created the Heaven and the earth”.

If you will notice it reads that God created the HEAVEN—NOT Heavens. Moses did not mention Heavens until Genesis Chapter 2:1 when God said, “Thus the Heavens and the earth were finished, and all the host of them”.

This is when God rested on the seventh day. Think about that for a few minutes.

There are many Heavens. Why did Moses, inspired by God, write Heaven? Just for a few moments let us think about our universe as being the earth, moon, sun, nine plus planets and the Milky Way Galaxy.

A planet and a star are different. A planet is like our nine plus planets and earth circling our Sun. A star is like our SUN. That means that all the stars you see in the Heaven at night probably all have other planets around them like our Sun. A star glows like our Sun. A planet does not glow like our Sun and all the stars in the Milky Way Galaxy.

Let us stop for a few minutes and all of us think about everything on this earth. In fact, yes, EVERYTHING has an END. We are born and then we die—an END. We go to the END of the room and there is a wall. We go to the END of the road, and it does END. We go to the deepest ocean or sea and there is a bottom. We burn wood, and that is the END of the wood (yes, the wood then changes into gases). Thank about it? There is an end to EVERYTHING on earth. Right? You MUST think about that for a moment! From childhood we are conditioned and taught that EVERYTHING has an END to it. We have accepted the FACT that there is an END to EVERYTHING on earth. I could use so many examples, but I think you get what I am trying to tell you?

I have read and understand that the earth is approximately 24,000 miles around it and then you END up where you started—an END. The earth is approximately 15,000 miles in diameter. You can go through the middle and you END up on the other side of the earth. Keep ALL this in mind when we compare it to the Heavens.

Now let us talk about the Heavens—more than one. There is no END. You do NOT go for millions or trillions of miles and then there is a wall or an END. THERE IS NOT AN END! That is just a simple way of trying to understand God. There is NO beginning and NO ENDING. When you think in terms of God, you CANNOT think in the same terms that we think here on earth. The most intelligent man or woman on earth CANNOT explain God. God is EVERYWHERE at the same time. God is GREATER than anything we can describe with words of our language. There are NO words in ALL the languages on earth that can describe God. YOU CANNOT DO IT!!! Just to say God is everlasting or almighty does not even begin to describe God. God has NO BEGINNING AND NO ENDING. Listen to me—GOD HAS NO BEGINNING AND NO ENDING. Do you understand? God has NO BEGINNING AND NO ENDING! With my earthy mind, I cannot even begin to understand or describe God. Maybe you feel that you can sufficiently describe God. I do NOT think so! If you think you can, you do NOT know the God I know. Expand your mind to think about someone you cannot describe. That is the God

I know. God is love. Yes, that is one small way to describe God. The God that you have always know cannot be described with our human mind or brain.

Let me see, if I can attempt to explain Heaven—NOT Heavens? Our Moon is approximately 240,000 miles from earth. Our Sun is approximately 93 million miles from earth. Beyond that we need to start measuring in Light Years. What does that mean? Light is the fastest thing we have on earth. A Light Year is how far light can travel in a year. Well, LIGHT travels 186,000 miles in one second, 11 million miles in one minute and 678 million miles in an hour. One LIGHT YEAR is 5,878,499,810,000 miles a light will travel in one year. Yes, that is 5 trillion, 878 billion miles in one year. Is that too much to think about? Then go back to seconds, minutes of hours. Our Milky Way Galaxy is approximately 100,000 Light Years (NOT MILES) wide. That would mean the Milky Way Galaxy is 58,749,981,000,000,000 miles wide. That is the Heaven that Moses, inspired by God, was talking about in the first book of the first chapter of the Bible (Genesis). I

am only talking about the Universe that God gave to us as human beings. It is more that we (humans) will ever explore. We as humans are just now talking about going to our nine plus planets. Remember what I said the difference is between a planet and a star?

We do not know how many STARS (not planets) are in our Milky Way Galaxy.

Guessing, I would have to say there are millions and millions?

PS: the closest Galaxy to our Milky Way Galaxy is Andromeda gal and that is 2,200,000 Light Years away—NOT MILES—from our Milky Way Galaxy. That is more than I can ever comprehend or even be able to understand.

I do not want to get so deep "in the weeds" that you will want to stop reading this book. PLEASE stay with me. After a little more reading, trust me, a light will go off in your head that will tell you what I am trying to put in your mind.

I know this is hard for you to get your mind around. I am writing this book and it is VERY

hard for me to TRY and understand. However, try to widen your mind and think in terms of NO END when it comes to God. Concentrate on NO ENDING for just a few moments. Our Earth is part of the moon, sun, nine plus planets and PLUS the Milky Way Galaxy. That is what God and the Lord created in seven days for us (humans).

It is easy to describe everything here on earth, but when it comes to Heaven we cannot. I do not believe there is anyone here on earth can comprehend or understand the true greatest of the Heavens or God. I cannot.

WE HAVE NO LANGUAGE TO DESCRIBE THE HEAVENS AND GOD.

SOMETIMES WHAT YOU ARE MOST AFRAID OF BELIEVING IS THE VERY THING THAT WILL SET YOU FREE.

Let me talk to all the atheists out in the world. First, I do not believe you are truly an atheist. Because, if you were on your death bed, and you knew it, somehow, I think you would pray or call on a super national power to help you.

That is God! If you were in unspeakable pain or hurting very, very badly, you would call or pray for someone to help you. That is God you are praying or asking to help you.

As an atheist, please explain to me how space does not have an END? Explain to me how the trillions of stars and planets do not run into each other? Why is there complete harmony in our universe? Do you know the reason you cannot explain these things? It is because you are NOT a real atheist. The ONLY WAY you can explain our universe in complete harmony is to admit that there is a God to control all of it. A God you may not know like I do.

Sorry for the last two paragraphs, but I have some friends that are atheist. Nothing would please me more than to see them believe in God because they are very precious friends of mine. They are wonderful people.

DO NOT LET AN IDEA RENT A SPACE IN YOUR HEAD, UNLESS IT IS THE CORRECT BRAIN WAVE.

Now let us go back to the first chapter and first verse of Genesis to find out how humans as we

know them today got started. Moses wrote: "In the beginning God created the Heaven (not Heavens) and the Earth". In the beginning as we know it today. God created ALL the Heavens. However, for now I want you to just think about God creating the Heaven and **Earth, then resting on the seventh day. I will explain more about this later.**

God's son, Jesus, came to earth to show us how to live and worship God. Jesus was teaching His disciples how to pray.

Matthew 6:9 "After this manner therefore pray ye: Our Father which art in Heaven, hallowed be Thy Name. (10) Thy kingdom come, THY (GOD) WILL BE DONE IN EARTH, AS IT IS IN HEAVEN (not Heavens)".

Our EARTH is very uniquely created. Some science says the EARTH is 15 billion years old, and maybe it is? However, our world, as we know it today, is approximately 6,000 years old. I will write more about our EARTH later.

MORNING STARTS AT MIDNIGHT WHILE IT IS STILL DARK. STAY WITH ME AND THE LIGHT (UNDERSTANDING) WILL COME TO YOU.

Okay, let me get this subject out of the way NOW! Yes, there were people and dinosaurs living on earth before Adam and Eve. The people were called Cave men and women. How did they get on earth? I do not know. I cannot believe they came from apes. If they did, why do we not have humans coming from apes NOW? Is it just someone's belief because they cannot explain how the Caves men got here on earth to begin with? All I know for SURE is ALL the Cave men dinosaurs, animals, plants and ALL life were DEAD when God came to earth and created Adam and Eve. Genesis 1:2-3 says;

"And the earth was without form, and void; and Darkness was upon the face of the deep. And the Spirit of God moved upon the face of the waters. (3)

And God said, let there be light: and there was light."

You see, without Light there could be no LIFE. No trees, animals, greenery no LIFE. All our oceans and seas out of control. (I will explain St John 1:4 in comparison to this verse later.) This is the time when God created Adam and Eve.

Moses inspired by God said in Genesis 1:26 to 28 to Adam and Eve to multiply and "REPLENISH" the earth.

"God said, let US make man in OUR image, after OUR likeness; and let them have dominion over the fish of the sea, and over the fowl of the air, and over the cattle, and over all the earth, and over every creeping thing that creeps upon the earth. (27) So, God created man in HIS OWN IMAGE, in the IMAGE of GOD CREATED HE HIM (humans); male and female created HE (God) them (humans). (28) And God blessed them, and God said unto them, be fruitful, and multiply, and 'REPLENISH' the earth".

How can you REPLENISH anything unless it was there before? When you RELENISH something, that means there was something there before. Yes, I believe in Cavemen and Dinosaurs. It has been proven, by science, with bones that they

lived thousands and millions of years ago on earth before Adam and Eve. Then some large disaster took place on earth, and ALL the Cavemen and Dinosaurs were destroyed (died). I guess they would not have been adaptable in our human race, as it is today. Many writers of the Bible are afraid to mention this is their books.

Just a 150 years ago, the ideas of Charles Darwin's writings in the "Origin of Species" was very popular. If you believe it, this is where you need to insert your evolution of men with the Caveman. Maybe man came from Apes or WHATEVER?

We DO NOT know how man arrived on earth then? There are many theories. The Bible choose not to tell us about what took place or happened BEFORE Adam and Eve. That is NOT the world we live in today! Science has come to grasp the fundamental truth recorded thousands of years ago in the book of Genesis. Our Universe as we know it today had a BEGINNING with Adam and Eve. Some very wise people think that a very large meteor came through our atmosphere

and hit the earth? That caused dust to rise and cover all the earth. All the waters uncontrolled and darkness was over all the earth. That would have destroyed all vegetation on earth. Therefore, all life on earth would have died. That, to me, does seems very possible? YOU MAKE YOUR OWN THEORY!

(Do you know that thousands of meteors hit our atmosphere every day and burn up before they reach the earth?)

When the earth was dark and had NO life on it, is when we begin the first of our Bible or OUR WORLD AS WE KNOW IT TODAY. You cannot say that the Bible is wrong because it tells us that Adam and Eve were the first people on earth as we know it now. The Bible and science prove that is correct.

ONE BIG UNIVERSE AND I HAVE THE PRIVILEGE OF COMMUNICATING WITH YOU.

Can we stop, just for a few moments, and think back over what we have talked about?

A. God created the Heaven and the Earth in six days for Adam and Eve, then He rested on the seventh day.
B. Everything on Earth has an END.
C. Everything dealing with the Heavens does not have a Beginning or Ending.
D. We talked about the size of our Universe and Heaven (and all the Heavens).
E. Do not even try to describe God.
    a. God described Himself one time as "I am".
    b. That is what we need to start saying to ourselves: I am happy, I am well, I am successful, I am at peace, etc.
F. Yes, there were Cavemen and Dinosaurs before Adam and Eve.
G. Everything was destroyed before God created Adam and Eve.
H. Questions, and more questions? Yes, they will all be answered.

Did you notice that God said to someone in Genesis Chapter 1:26? "God said, Let US make man in OUR image, after OUR likeness".

WHO WAS GOD TALKING TOO? Jesus was there with God. Wait before you say "no". I will PROVE it later in many places in the Bible.

A lot of people would like to try and describe God. The only way I can look at this is on the sixth day God said LET US create man in OUR OWN IMAGE. That is when HE created Adam. Is that hard to understand? If you want to see or have an idea of how God looks, then look at a human—any human. We are created in the image and likeness of God. Look in the mirror. DO YOU HEAR WHAT I AM SAYING? We look like God and God looks like us. When God spoke to Jesus and said; "Let us (God and Jesus) make man in our likeness".

Yes, God is in a spiritual world, and we are in a physical/human world. Yes, yes, yes… However, how many times have you heard, "what does God look like?" I need to repeat it again. Let me say that we look like God and God looks like us. The difference is we are in the human world and God is in the spiritual world.

Sorry ladies, but Adam came first. After Adam was created God said that Adam needed a soul

mate. That is when God put Adam to sleep and took one of his ribs to create a woman.

Genesis 2:21 "And the LORD God caused a deep sleep to fall upon Adam, and he slept; and He took one of his ribs and closed up the flesh instead thereof. (22) And the rib, which the LORD God had taken from man, made Him a Woman, and brought her unto the man".

Notice the Bible said; "LORD God". More about this later.

Yes, God said that Adam and Eve were as one. They became as one. When you get married the minister says to the man and woman that you are as one. God and his Son, Jesus, are as one. Sorry, it might be hard to except how two beings (human and spiritual) can be one, but this is the way it is. Just accept it. We are TWO beings. However, we are as one. Open your mind and believe it. Accept it. There are many things in life we must accept. They are true even if it is hard for us to accept.

**ONE OF THE
HARDEST THINGS
TO DO IN LIFE
IS LETTING GO OF WHAT
YOU THOUGHT WAS
REAL.**

St John 1:18 says; "No man hath SEEN God (the Father) at ANY time; the only Begotten Son (Jesus), which is in the bosom of the Father, He (Jesus) hath declared Him".

St John 6:38 says; "For I (Jesus) came DOWN from Heaven, not to do Mine own will, but the will of Him (the Father) that sent me". (41) "The Jews then murmured at Him (Jesus), because He said, I am the Bread which came DOWN from Heaven". (46) "Not that any man hath seen the Father, save He (Jesus) which is of God, He (Jesus) hath seen the Father". (62) "What and if ye shall see the Son of man (Jesus) ascend up WHERE HE (Jesus) WAS BEFORE?"

Am I getting you to open your eyes even a little? Maybe a little more?

St John 1:10; "He (Jesus) was in the world, and the world (earth) was MADE by Him (Jesus), and the world knew Him (Jesus) not".

St John 1:15 says; "John (the Baptist) bare witness of Him (Jesus), and cried; saying, 'This was He (Jesus) of whom I spoke. He (Jesus) that cometh after me is preferred before me: for HE (Jesus) WAS BEFORE ME'. (1:30) This is He (Jesus) of whom I said; After me cometh a Man which is preferred before me: For He (Jesus) was BEFORE me".

St Luke 1:34-37 "Then said Mary (Jesus' mother) unto the angel, 'how shall this be, seeing I know not a man'? (35) And the angel answered and said unto her. The Holy Spirit shall come upon thee, and the power of the Highest shall overshadow thee; therefore, also that Holy thing which shall be born of thee shall be called the Son of God. (Jesus was/IS the "Son of God"—not the SON of Joseph) (36) And, behold, thy cousin Elisabeth (John the Baptist' mother) hath also conceived a son in her old age; and this is the sixth month with her, who was called barren. (37) For with God nothing shall be impossible".

Remember Mary (Jesus' Mother) went to Elizabeth's home to take care of her when she was with child. Mary and Elizabeth were cousins. John the Baptist was born SIX months BEFORE Jesus. Jesus and John were cousins. John the Baptist knew when Jesus was born. Then John the Baptist said in the verse before this; "Jesus came AFTER Him (John the Baptist)". Jesus was born SIX months after John the Baptist. However, John the Baptist then said but "HE (Jesus) WAS BEFORE ME". The Baptist repeated it again in verse (30). What did John the Baptist mean? He was saying Jesus was before him when He (Jesus) created the world as we know it today. Elizabeth must have known Jesus was the Savior of the Jews. John the Baptist MUST have known. However, he did not believe it until Jesus came to him to be baptized. That is when John saw the Spirit of God like a Dove come over Jesus and remained there. Confused? Sorry.

St John 1:29 "John (the Baptist) saw Jesus coming unto him, and said, Behold the LAMB of God, which taketh away the sin of the world. (31) And I knew Him not: but that He should be made manifest to Israel, therefore am I come

baptizing with water. (32) And John bare record, saying, I saw the Spirit descending from Heaven like a Dove, and it abode upon Him. (33) And I knew Him not; but He that sent me to baptize with water, the same said unto me, 'upon whom thou shalt see the Spirit descending, and remaining on Him, the same is He which will baptize with the Holy Spirit' (34) And I saw, and bare record that this is the Son of God. (36) Looking upon Jesus as He walked, he (John the Baptist) said, behold the lamb of God!"

Notice the Bible said in verse 1:29, 36 John (the Baptist) called Jesus the LAMB of God?

Repeating, St John 1:29 "Behold the LAMB of God, which taketh away the sin of the world". John not only looked at Jesus as the Son of God, but he also looked at Jesus as the LAMB of God. This could only be because John the Baptist knew of the prophecies throughout the Bible telling of our Savior and Christ being offered as a LAMB of God for OUR sins and healings.

Think about this for a few moments. Jesus was a man raised among His friends and relatives, and they did not know that HE was our Lord

Jesus Christ? It was only after Jesus started His ministry that God revealed Jesus to the world. John the Baptist's eyes were open when John baptized Jesus. The Jews and priest in St John 6:42 "said, is not this Jesus, the Son of Joseph, whose father and mother we know?" JESUS WAS "NOT" THE SON OF JOSEPH. JESUS WAS/IS THE "SON OF GOD". IF JESUS WERE THE SON OF JOSEPH, HE (JESUS) WOULD BE LIKE ONE OF US. JESUS WAS/IS THE "SON OF GOD!!!" JESUS IS "MUCH MORE" THAN YOU OR I COULD EVER BE!!! DO YOU HEAR ME, JESUS IS MUCH MORE!!!

Remember what I mentioned to you before about three (3) meaning the Godhead. Jesus was approximately 30 when He begin His Ministry. Jesus taught the world for about three (3) years before He died on the cross.

Now approximately 2,000 years later we are still accepting Him as our Lord Jesus Christ. Every seventh day we attend church, we accept Jesus as Christ. Each time we pray, we are accepting Jesus as our Christ. After 2,000 years why do millions of people not believe Jesus as OUR Lord Jesus Christ? I do not know the answer.

However, millions of people do accept Jesus, as Christ, even though Jesus just ministered for three years. Jesus is the most outstanding human EVER to live here on earth. There is no one that ever came close to being as important, to all of us, as Jesus. Jesus help create human beings. Then He came to Earth to help us even more. Every day I live, I thank Jesus even more for all He has done and is doing for all of us. Thank you, Jesus...

In this writing as many other books, TV shows, movies, etc. people are trying to get you to believe that Jesus IS OUR Lord and Christ.

I feel most of you have no idea Who you are praying to, when you pray to our Lord Jesus Christ?

Jesus is LIFE and the LIFE is and was the Light of men (and women). Did you read that I wrote Jesus is LIFE? Several times I hope to prove that Jesus is the only One that could die for our sins. Jesus was the only One that rose from the dead, after being completely dead. Jesus is the One and only One born at One BC and AD.

Jesus is the only One that taught us for three years. Now it has lasted for over 2000 years. Jesus is the only One to over-come Satan. Jesus is the One all the Holy men in the Bible talked about for 4000 before He came to Earth. Jesus is the only One to show us how to live. Jesus is the only One born of a virgin. In this book I will prove all of this and MORE. Jesus is much more than all the things I just spoke about. Jesus is much more than I could ever describe to you. Jesus is much more than you or I will ever understand. I cannot begin to describe all the things about Jesus. I cannot even describe all the things Jesus did while He lived here in the world. However, I am going to try and tell you things about Jesus that are true. Some of you might not believe them. Some of you might shake your head and say; "how can that be true?" I do not know how it is true, but it is. Remember, Jesus is God also. We have the Father (God), Lord (Jesus Christ) and the Holy Spirit. Once you are, able to believe and accept that, we have moved to a very good beginning. I am going to get you to believe that Jesus is our EVERYTHING. Jesus was not just a Holy Man when He lived here on earth. Jesus was with

God in the beginning. I will NEVER get tired of talking about how wonderful Jesus is. But, enough of that for now.

I will be the first one to say, "I do not understand everything in the Bible". I do not comprehend everything that God does. However, I do except everything that is written in the Bible. That is all I am trying to explain to you. IF YOU DO NOT BELIEVE IN THE BIBLE OR A SUPREME POWER, IT IS GOING TO BE HARD FOR YOU TO ACCEPT SOME OF THE THINGS I AM TELLING YOU. Please TRY to accept what I am expressing to you from my heart.

The four Gospels, in the New Testament, and other books in the Bible were written by men several years after Jesus Christ died and rose again from death. Jesus was alive, as a human, on earth for 40 days after His Crucifixion. Then He accented into Heaven while hundreds of people were watching Him.

For example, the book of St Matthew was written approximately four years (A.D. 37) after Christ rose from the dead. The events recorded in St Mathew cover a period of 38

years. St Mark was written approximately 24 or more years after Jesus rose from the death (between A.D. 57 and 63). The events recorded in his book cover a period of seven (7) years. St Luke approximately 33 years after Jesus rose from the dead (between A.D. 63 and 68). The events recorded in his book cover a period of 39 years. Then there is St John that wrote the Gospel all the way to approximately 52 years later (between A.D. 85 and 90). The events recorded in this book cover a period of seven (7) years. Then St John also wrote the book of Revelations about 63 years (A.D. 96) after Jesus rose from the dead. The four Gospels were all written after Jesus Christ was crucified and then rose from the dead. In fact, ALL the books in the New Testament were written after Jesus died and rose again.

St John 14:26 "but the Comforter, which is the Holy Ghost (Spirit), whom the Father (God) will send in My (Jesus) Name, He, shall teach you all things, and BRING ALL THINGS to your REMEMBRANCE, whatsoever I (Jesus) have SAID UNTO YOU".

St John 15:26 "when the Comforter (Holy Spirit) is come, whom I (Jesus) will send unto you from the Father (God), even the Spirit of truth, which proceeds from the Father, He (Holy 36 Spirit) shall testify of Me (Jesus)".

The Holy Spirit is who we should use to pray to Jesus Christ and God.

Let us go all the way back to King David in Psalms chapter 31. At the beginning of the chapter David said; (31:1) "In thee, O Lord, do I put my trust; let me never be ashamed: deliver me in thy righteousness." Then David ends the chapter with; (31:23-24) "O love the Lord, all ye his saints: for the Lord preserves the faithful, and plentifully rewards the proud doer. (24) Be of good courage, and He shall strengthen your heart, all ye that hope in the Lord." Remember, God had not yet sent the Holy Spirit. Jesus prayed and asked God to send us another Comforter. David faith was so strong in the Lord, that God comforted David by his Faith in the Lord. Go back and read St John 14:26 and St John 15:26; then when we pray, we should pray through the Comforter (Holy Spirit) that Jesus prayed to God to send to us.

(THIS BOOK IS MY OPION. PLEASE LET ME TRY TO EXPLAIN.)

EXPLAIN TO YOUR MIND
ABOUT THINGS
YOU HAVE NEVER THOUGHT
OR BELIEVED BEFORE!
OPEN YOUR MIND!

Let us go to St John chapter 1, verse one. "In the beginning was the WORD..." This is NOT talking about the Bible. The Bible was NOT written at the time. The WORD is describing Jesus. The WORD was not just a thought. Because the WORD was made Flash and dwelt among us. Keep this in mind as you read below.

"In the beginning was the --------------------------------- Word (Jesus), and the -- Word was, with God and the -- Word was God. (2) The -- same (Word) was in the beginning with God.

(3) All things were made by ------------------ Him (God and Jesus); and

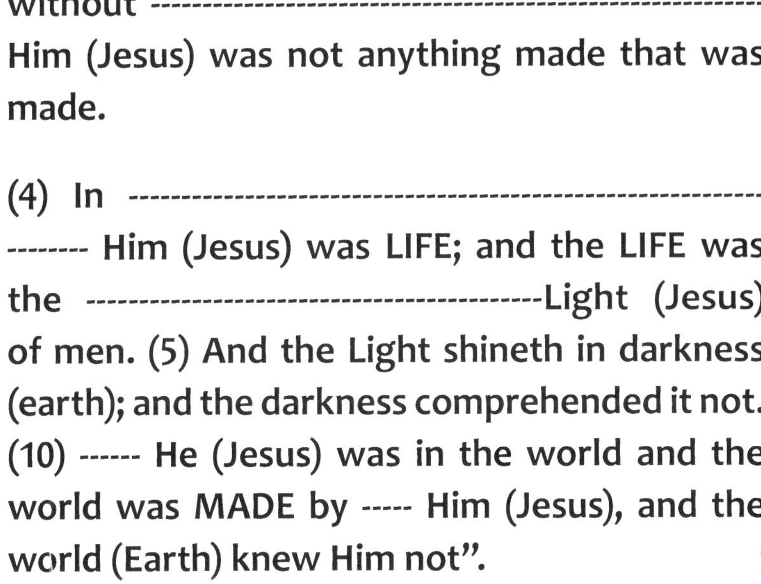

without -- Him (Jesus) was not anything made that was made.

(4) In --- -------- Him (Jesus) was LIFE; and the LIFE was the --Light (Jesus) of men. (5) And the Light shineth in darkness (earth); and the darkness comprehended it not. (10) ------ He (Jesus) was in the world and the world was MADE by ----- Him (Jesus), and the world (Earth) knew Him not".

St John could only call Jesus the Word in the beginning. Jesus had not become Jesus until Jesus was born on earth. St John was trying to explain Jesus as the WORD, LIFE and LIGHT. St John was writing what the Holy Spirit of God was inspiring him to write. In Jesus was LIFE; that is how Jesus breathed into Adam the breath of LIFE, and he became a living soul.

This is one of many verses in the Bible that helps to explain Jesus and where He came from.

St John 3:13 "No man hath ascended up to Heaven, but HE that CAME DOWN from Heaven, even the Son of man (Jesus) which is in Heaven".

St John had a very clear and unique insight of Jesus (God's Son), God (Father) and the Holy Ghost (Spirit of God). How much clearer does it need to be? I know that some people say that Jesus (God's Son) was like a thought in God's mind when He created the world. In my opinion Jesus (the Word) was more than a thought in the beginning. Jesus was in the beginning to help God create the earth as we know it today.

Let me insert this now! No, I do not believe in "reincarnation" with humans on earth. However, God can do anything. The way most people believe in reincarnation, is you need to be born on earth first as a human, then die and come back as another human or animal or whatever they believe reincarnation to be.

Jesus was like God in Heaven before He came to earth. Jesus was born without the assistance of a man.

St Matthew 1:23 "Behold a VIRGIN shall be with child, and shall bring forth a Son (Jesus), and they shall call His name Emmanuel, which being interpreted is, GOD WITH US".

Pay close attention to what St John says in the next verse.

St John 5:37 "The Father (God) Himself, which hath sent Me (Jesus), hath borne witness of Me. You have NEITHER HEARD HIS VOICE AT ANY TIME, NOR SEEN HIS (GOD) SHAPE".

Maybe we should ask "who talked to Adam and Eve in the Garden"? Could it have been Jesus? It had to be Jesus! Jesus had not been born on earth at that time. Then Jesus was referred to as "Lord God".

Genesis 3:8 "They (Adam and Eve) heard the voice of the Lord God walking in the garden in the cool of the day".

Most of the time in the Bible we refer to Jesus, we also refer to Him as Lord. Think about what was just said in St John and Genesis. The LORD (Jesus) GOD went walking in the garden to find

Adam and Eve. I could almost write a whole book about this subject only. Someday I might. You know the story about Adam and Eve hiding from the Lord God because they had sinned by disobedience to God. The Lord God has always wanted us to choose the future of our lives. He wants us to make our own decisions. Many humans seem to always make the wrong decisions. It is sad! Did you notice that Adam and Eve did not NOTICE they were naked until their disobedience to God?

If their disobedience had never happened, would we be walking around nude today? Maybe in a PERFECT world? I was just curious as to what you thought about it. More about DISOBEDIANCE later.

After Jesus had risen from the dead, Jesus showed Himself to His disciples many times. Once Jesus foretold St Peter's future in St John 21:18-19. Jesus said to St Peter; "When you were young that you dressed yourself, and walked where you wanted to go, but when you get old. Thou shall stretch forth thy hands and another shall dress you. And carry you where you would

NOT want to go. (19) This spoke Jesus, signifying what death Peter should glorify God".

Peter had been in prison before he was put to death, and they dressed him. He also went where he did NOT want to go. St Peter stretched out his hands, and they crucified him. He insisted on his crucifixion being upside down. This was his request. Peter did NOT feel worthy to be crucified like Jesus. How did Jesus know St Peter would live to be 68 years old? He was born 1BC, and died 67 AD. St Peter ministered for 34 years.

Almost all the Apostles were killed by stoning, crucifixion, etc. How did Jesus know that St Peter and St John would live to be very old?

Let me talk to you about St John for a few minutes. He wrote the book of Revelation (a prediction of things to come) and the last book in the Bible. God used St John in a special way. He had a uniquely different outlook of God, Jesus and the Holy Spirit. St John repeated what Jesus said in;

St John 14:16 "I (Jesus) will pray the Father (God), and He SHALL give you another Comforter

(Holy Spirit), that He MAY abide with you FOR EVER (two words to emphasize); (17) even the Spirit of truth, whom the world cannot receive, because it sees Him NOT, neither know Him: but ye know Him; for He dwelleth WITH YOU, and SHALL BE IN YOU."

Someday I might write a book just on St John and his insight and revelation of God, Jesus and the Holy Spirit.

The Holy Spirit of God gives us (you and me) the Spirit of TRUTH. Remember Jesus said: "He MAY abide with you forever". You need to allow the Holy Spirit to abide with you.

God, Jesus and the Holy Spirit are in the spiritual world, and we are in the human world. When we pray, we are trying to communicate to the spiritual world. Does that make any sense? You will have to trust the Holy Spirit to communicate for us to Jesus and God. Jesus SAID He would give us another Comforter to abide and communicate with Jesus for us. You will have to trust me that this is the way it works. It is the only way it works! We as sinful humans cannot communicate directly with Jesus or God. Look at

it like this—Jesus is Lord and God to us humans. I showed you earlier that NO MAN HAS EVER SEEN OR HEARD GOD.

Let us go back to the first of this book:

A. The First Day God separated Day from Night.
B. The Second Day God separated Vapor above and Water below.
C. The Third Day God separated Land & Sea also Plant Life appeared.
D. Fourth Day God created the Sun, Moon & Milky Way Galaxy.
E. Fifth Day God created Animal Life.
F. Sixth Day God created Man & Woman in His own Image.
G. Seventh Day God claimed it to be the Sabbath and He rested.

Notice that NO place did I say God had a hammer, screwdriver, nails or etc. How did God in seven days create the earth, sun, planets, moon, plants, animal life and man (plus woman)? Can you think about how He created ALL of this? God created ALL of it with WORDS! How can

you do that? How can ANYTHING like this be created with WORDS? God did!

I AM REALLY TRYING TO GET YOU TO THINK ABOUT THIS.

Think about how many times Jesus said in the Bible.

"ASK, (WORDS) and it shall be given you; SEEK, and you shall find; KNOCK, and it shall be opened unto you; (8) for every one that ASK receive; and he that SEEK find; and to him that KNOCK it shall be opened." (Matthew 7:7). "'I say unto you,' ASK, and it shall be given you; SEEK and ye shall find; KNOCK, and it shall be opened unto you. (10) For every one that ASK receive; and he that SEEKETH find; and he that KNOCHETH it shall be opened" (Luke 11:9-10). "Whatsoever we ASK, we receive of Him, because we keep His commandments, and do those things that are pleasing in His sight" (I John 3:22). "If any of you lack wisdom, let him ASK of God, that giveth to ALL men liberally, and upbraid not; and it SHALL be given him" (James 1:5).

Words...? Is that all it takes to get something from God? All I can try to get you to think about is God created the Heaven, earth, man and all that He created with WORDS. Believe it or not, God has told us we can do the same. We are created in the IMAGE and LIKENESS of God.

John was with Jesus when Jesus spoke these WORDS and said: (St John chapter 13, verses 13 & 14)

"Whatsoever you shall ASK (words) in My (Jesus) Name, that will I do, that the Father may be glorified in the Son (Jesus). (14) If you shall ASK (words) ANYTHING in My (Jesus) Name, I WILL DO IT".

Before we go forward, please let me point out something in the above verse from St John that you might have not noticed, "that the Father may be glorified in the Son". If you have an idea to ASK God for you to win the Powerball, make SURE "that the Father (God) may be glorified in the Son (Jesus)". If you win?

Before we go forward, another thing I need to point out. God does not need your money or

possessions. God already owns all of it. When we GIVE to God, it is not because God needs it. We give so we can be blessed. Understand?

LET ME MAKE IT PERFECTLY CLEAR! GOD, JESUS OR THE HOLY SPIRIT ARE NOT OUR SERVENTS. Sometimes you might ASK and NOT receive. That DOES NOT mean that you cannot JUST ASK AND RECEIVE. God wants you to RECEIVE.

Several times I have asked the Lord for something and did not get it. I started telling myself that the Lord says to me YES, NO or NOT AT THIS TIME. Several times I have asked the Lord for something and I got something else. Later I realized that what He gave me was better for me than what I asked for. I am not trying to make excuses. I am trying to get you to OPEN your mind. I am trying to tell you how real life is sometimes. I am trying to tell you that if you really want something bad enough to ASK and be willing to keep ASKING until you get it. Many of us give up when we do not get what we want and when we want it. Again, let me SAY THAT GOD IS NOT OUR SERVENT TO WAIT ON US WHEN AND HOW WE WANT SOMETHING.

KEEP WALKING THROUGH THE STORM. YOUR RAINBOW IS WAITING ON THE OTHER SIDE.

Now back to St John, inspired by God, wrote in chapter 15 verses 7 & 8 that Jesus said:

"If you abide in Me (Jesus), and My WORDS abide in you, you shall ASK (words) what you will, and it shall be done unto you. (8) Herein is My Father glorified that you bear much fruit; so, shall you be my disciples."

Remember that "herein is my Father glorified". In verse eight, ALL Jesus is asking that you bear MUCH FRUIT. What does "much fruit" mean? The Bible tells us that ALL we need to do is bear fruit. What does that mean?

Galatians 5:22 "The FRUIT of the Spirit is love, joy, peace, longsuffering, gentleness, goodness, faith, (23) meekness, temperance: against such there is no law".

You should have these “Fruits of the Spirit” in your life, even if, you do not believe in God or Jesus. With these “Fruit of the Spirit” in your life, “you shall ASK what you will, and it shall be done unto you”. That is worth repeating. Jesus is NOT asking something impossible of you.

Jesus is just asking that you have the “Fruits of the Spirit” in your life. IS THAT HARD FOR YOU OR ME TO DO? It is NOT for me!

LOVE IS THE GREATEST OF THE “FRUIT OF THE SPIRIT”. “GOD IS LOVE”. That is worth saying again—I John 4:8 “He that loveth not, does not know God; for God is love”.

AT THE END OF THIS BOOK I WILL TRY AND EXPLAIN, IN MY OPINION, WHAT LOVE REALLY IS. I WILL CALL IT, “THE CIRCLE OF LOVE”.

IS ANY OF THIS GETTING THROUGH TO YOU? What else do I need to say? How can I convince you that you can create ANYTHING with WORDS?

We need to talk about something. If you are a Christian, Jew, atheist or whatever you believe in, you need to trust God or at least believe there

is a higher power. This higher power created and controls the universe that we live in. This is only a starting point. If you do not believe in God, I beg you too, at least, consider what I am trying to tell you. It might work for you.

YOUR EYES ARE USELESS WHEN THE MIND IS BLIND.

Jesus tried to explain to Nicodemus, a very rich and religious man in the Bible that the Spirit of God is like the wind (St John 3:8 to 10).

"The wind blows where it listens, and thou hear the sound thereof, but cannot tell whence it cometh, and whither it goes; so is every one that is born of the spirit. (9) Nicodemus answered and said unto him, how can these things be? (10) Jesus answered and said unto him, art thou a master of Israel, and know not these things?"

You cannot see where it comes from or where it goes, but you feel it. You know it is there. I think it would be hard for you to say that you do not feel the wind. Maybe by faith you can accept some of what I trying to tell you in this book as being true.

If you do not believe anything that I have written at the first of this book, you must be one of the people that still believe the earth is flat?

Maybe, I can put all of this in your hands, so you can explain to me how many things work?

A. How can all the planets and stars revolve around and not run into the other ones?
B. Why do we have the sun show its face every day with daylight and warmth while it is approximately 93 million miles away?
C. Why does the moon at night shine from a reflection of the sun, and why does the moon control the tides of all the oceans and seas?
D. Why do we have spring, summer, fall and winter every year?
E. Why do all the plants and animals on earth reproduce after their same type?
F. How can a man and a woman reproduce and make a baby like them?
G. Why are there so many things that happen on earth that we cannot explain?

I know sometimes it is hard for us to believe in something that we cannot see. Even believe in a God that we cannot physically see. Even believe in Jesus that we do not even know the exact day, week or month He was born, or have an

exact picture or drawing of Him. However, we must accept Him by faith.

Faith is something you must believe even though you cannot see it. Something you accept even though there is a doubt. Let me try to explain it in this way: Faith is a visualization and belief of attainment of your desire. Faith is the main chemistry of the mind. When Faith is mixed with thought, the subconscious mind instantly picks up on the vibration, translates it in its spiritual equivalent, and transmits it to a Higher Intelligence, as in the case of prayer.

If this book will cause you to read the Bible more, I feel I have accomplished the goal of writing this it.

THERE ARE NO LIMITATIONS TO THE MIND ACCEPT THOSE WE ACKNOWLEDGE.

You believe in things every day. When you turn on the light switch that the lights will come on. When you go to sleep, you believe you will wake up the next morning. When you talk, you can communicate with someone else with words. You even believe the sun will come up every morning and give you light and warmth for you and the world. You believe that every night it will get dark and night will come. You believe if you do not eat you will starve to death. THERE ARE SO MANY THINGS WE BELIEVE IN OUR EVERYDAY LIFE THAT WE TAKE FOR GRANTED. Just think for a few minutes. I am sure you can name hundreds of them. Take a few moments and see how many you can name.

YOU MUST BELIEVE IN GOD THE SAME WAY. When God says something, YOU MUST BELIEVE IT.

Now let me change the subject.

CAN YOU BROADEN YOUR MIND TO SOMETHING DIFFERENT?

Adam and Eve were created approximately six thousand years ago. Why do you think Adam was created approximately 4,000 BC? Adam was not created one (1) BC or one (1) AD. Let us refer to BC as before Jesus Christ, and AD as after Jesus Christ for now. For 4,000 years before Jesus all the men of God were predicting that Jesus was coming to earth. Is it not strange that Jesus was born on ONE BC and ONE AD, after God's chosen people talked about Him coming for 4,000 years? Do you not think that God planned it this way? YES!

One third of the Bible is filled with Prophecies telling of things to come.

Since Jesus was born, approximately 2,000 years have passed. In the Bible it was spoked of the Millennium as being 1,000 years. The Millennium is when we all live with Jesus Christ on earth a 1,000 year in peace. After this we have no account of what will take place.

This is 2019. That is approximately 2019 years since Jesus was born. Approximately 1,986, since Jesus died at 33 A.D? Remember seven means COMPLETION in the Bible. Remember the "Lord God created the Heaven and earth in six days and rested on the seventh".

Now let us go back and add. From Adam to Jesus was about 4,000 years. From Jesus to now is approximately 2,000 years. The Millennium is 1,000 years. All of these added up equals 7,000 years. All of us should see that this is God's PERFECT plan!

As a footnote, approximately every 2,000 years in our history something outstanding has happened. About 2,000 years after Adam and Eve the great flood came and killed all the people living on earth except Noah and his family. All of mankind had to start over again because the human race had become so evil. The Lord God placed a Rainbow in the sky as a sign that He would never destroy the earth with a flood like this again.

From Adam until Noah some MEN lived almost a thousand years. Methuselah, Nosh's

grandfather, lived to be 969. He was the oldest person mentioned in the Bible. Interesting enough, Methuselah died the same year that the Lord God judged the sinful world with the flood of Noah's day.

Then after the flood the Lord God promised the humans 100 years of life. There are a few that have gone beyond 100 years. However, the Lord God promised us 100 years after the Flood. I personally hope to make it to 100 years old.

Jesus was born approximately 2,000 years after the world-wide flood. If you believe the Bible as predicted approximately 2,000 years after the birth of Jesus that He will come back to earth again. According to the Bible, that is when we live on earth for a thousand years with Jesus in peace. As far as how many people will live with Christ for a--1000 years, I do not know? ONLY Christ can judge. We CANNOT judge. All we know are the things that God wants us to know.

Jesus lived on earth approximately 33 years. The Holy Spirit did not come until after Jesus died, rose from the dead and returned to God.

This is when Jesus said; "I will pray the Father and He shall give you another Comforter"—the Holy Spirit. Jesus did not start His ministry until He was approximately 30 years old. Jesus ministered for approximately three years. Remember what THREE means—the Godhead (Father, Son and Holy Spirit). Can you believe that Jesus just ministered for approximately three years and His WORD and ministry has lasted for over 2,000 years? Jesus is known by more people now than He was 2,000 years ago.

Jesus was God that came to earth to show us how to live. We as humans must see things, before we believe them. Well, the men that wrote the New Testament did see Jesus. Jesus was a man that lived on earth like us. Jesus had all the same temptations we have. Jesus ate food like we do. Jesus slept like we do. Yet Jesus DID NOT SIN.

Remember at the beginning of this book we said that the Lord God created everything including Adam and Eve in six days and then He rested on the seven day?

Keep that in your mind.

If I were a betting man, I would bet some of the things I have said and some of the things I will say that you have NEVER heard before?

FORM YOU OWN OPINION OF THE NEXT THINGS I AM GOING TO TELL YOU.

Back to the Bible in II Peter Chapter 3 verse 8, Peter said;

"beloved, be not ignorant of this one thing, that one day is with the Lord as a thousand years, and a thousand years as one day".

Was Peter trying to tell us that God created the earth and all that is in it in six thousand years and then rested for a thousand years? Probably not true? I DO NOT KNOW? It would NOT make any difference to me.

Adam & Eve 2,000 years to Noah 2,000 years to Jesus 2,000 years to Present Millennium 1,000 years After ???? years

All the above years are 7,000—God's perfect plan. Remember that seven in the Bible stands for completion.

We have no record or idea what happens after being with Christ Jesus for the 1,000--year Millennium. I feel we will be with Him throughout eternity.

(STAY WITH ME—WE HAVE JUST STARTED)

However, I know that God has a PREFECT plan for us starting with Adam and Eve. I know that throughout the Bible six (6) is referred to MAN. Seven (7) is always referred to as COMPLETE. Three (3) is always referred to as the GODHEAD.

If you believe the Bible, and I hope you do. Before Christ returns to earth the antichrist is referred to with 666. Remember MAN is referred to with SIX (6). GODHEAD is referred to with THREE (3). A man (6) on earth tries to copy God (3), therefore the Bible refers to the antichrist as 666. A man on earth trying to say he is god (6—3 times). Whooooooo! That is the reason he is referred to as the anti-Christ. Numbers mean something in the Bible and in our everyday life. Our whole system and computers on earth runs with numbers. (More about this later).

Please answer a question for me: For 4,000 years after Adam and Eve to Jesus, men offered an animal sacrifice to God to cover their sins? All families that lived and worshipped God offered a sacrifice. Normally it was the best spotless lame that they owned.

Notwithstanding that thought, please show me ONE place in the Bible after Jesus Christ was crucified that someone offered a sacrifice? You see Jesus Christ was the SUPREME SACRIFICE. There was no need for a sacrifice after Jesus Christ, the Son of God, was sacrificed (crucified). Can you answer that question for me? We do NOT offer a sacrifice lame on the altar of God now for the forgiveness of our sins. I would be willing to guess the devil himself cannot answer this question?

I have heard people say; "if God is so LOVING, why did He allow Jesus to die on the cross"? GOD DID NOT! YOU AND I CAUSED JESUS TO DIE ON THE CROSS! We caused Jesus to die because of OUR DISOBEDIENCE and SIN before GOD! It was NOT something that God did. It was something

that WE DID. Jesus died for OUR DISOBEDIENCE and SIN—NOT HIS! Yes; St John 3:16

"For God so loved the world, that He GAVE His only begotten Son, that whosoever believeth in Him SHOULD NOT perish, but have everlasting life".

Do you really believe that Jesus' beginning was as a Human Baby? No.

I do NOT want to leave this thought for now. Is there ANY way you can see that YOU and I caused Jesus to die on the cross? Whether you believe it or not, IT IS TRUE! God did NOT want His Son to die on the cross! DO NOT LOOK AT GOD AND SAY GOD ALOWED IT! NO, YOU AND I ALLOWED IT! YOU AND I CAUSED IT! IF WE DID NOT DISOBEY GOD AND SIN, JESUS WOULD NOT HAVE HAD TO DIE ON THE CROSS! Sorry, but I have heard so many people say; "how can a merciful God allow Jesus to die like He did? GOD DID NOT! YOU AND I DID! DO YOU HEAR WHAT I AM SAYING—YOU AND I CAUSED JESUS TO DIE ON THE CROSS! Sorry, but I NEEDED to say that one more time—YOU AND I CAUSED JESUS TO DIE ON THE CROSS!

THINK ABOUT THAT FOR A FEW MINUTES???

If you and I lived righteous for a thousand years, we would still NOT be worthy to go to Heaven. We are going to Heaven because of our Lord Jesus Christ.

The Bible contains 66 books. Six (6) represents man, and the Bible was written by men inspirited by God. No, I do not believe the Dead Sea Scrolls belong in the Bible. If they belonged in the Bible, they would be in the Bible. Several people wrote books during the time of Jesus Christ, and they are not in the Bible. Every word in the Bible is inspired my God even though it was written by a man. Every word can be explained. There are no mistakes.

Some of the things I have been writing are different and I am sure you have not heard it in the past. Please DO NOT dislike me for it. I am just trying to get you to think about the Bible in a different way.

From Adam and Eve to Jesus the world was ruled by LAW. From Jesus to our time the world is ruled by LOVE.

**IT IS POSSIBLE
TO GIVE AND NOT LOVE,
BUT IMPOSSIBLE
TO LOVE AND NOT GIVE.**

(Please think about that for a moment.)I love you as a human being and just want you to open your mind to God and think about Jesus, Heaven and the spiritual things differently. I AM NOT saying the things you have always heard about the Bible are wrong. All I am trying to do is EXPAND your mind about God, Jesus and the Bible. You are the ONLY one who can control your mind. It is an awesome responsibility.

**IF YOU HELP ENOUGH PEOPLE
GET WHAT THEY WANT IN LIFE,
I BELIEVE YOU CAN GET
EVERYTHING YOU WANT IN LIFE.**

I am trying to get you curious enough about the Bible until you will want to study it more. Find out things about it that you never knew before. Be inspired to talk to others about the most important book THAT HAS EVER BEEN WRITTEN.

I want to tell you a story about a very good friend of mind. This lady did not like her husband's relatives. She called me by phone and had her husband on the extension. I did not know he was on the phone also. Her husband's sister just died, and she was never baptized in water. My friend had been told, her entire life, that you must be baptized in water to go to Heaven. My friend wanted me to convince her husband that his sister did not go to Heaven when she died because she had not been baptized in water. Sad...

Earlier in this book I was talking about a man in the Bible called Nicodemus. Therefore, I turn in the Bible to St John 3:1

"Nicodemus, a ruler of the Jews came to Jesus by night and said unto Him, Rabbi, (they called Jesus TEACHER, more than they called Him Savior) we know that you are a teacher come from God for no man can do these miracles that you do, except God be with him. (3) Jesus answered and said unto him, verity, verity, I say unto thee. Except a man be born again, he cannot see the kingdom of God. (5) Jesus

said, except a man be born of WATER and of the SPIRIT, He cannot enter into the kingdom of God".

She said; "see"?

Then, I said to her; "wait"! Have you ever seen a baby born? The mother carries the baby for nine months in a bag of water. What happens after a mother's water breaks? Then she gives birth, and a child is BORN. We are first born of water then we must be born of the Spirit—SECOND. Remember, Nicodemus said; "how can I be born again?" That is when Jesus tried to explain to him about the Spirit of God. Jesus said; "the Spirit is like the wind, it blows and you feel it, but you do not know from whence it comes or where it goes". Let me say that again! We live in the physical world and God lives in a Spiritual world. You should accept the Spirit of God to get in touch with the Lord Jesus Christ. St John 14:16 says;

"I (Jesus) will pray the Father, and He (God) shall give you another Comforter (Holy Spirit), that He MAY abide with you forever. (17) Even the Spirit of truth."

Baptizing is a way of following the teachings of Jesus. You go down in the water, like in the grave, then you rise from the grave as a new person. It is an example, ONLY.

Remember, when Jesus was hanging on the cross between two criminals. One cursed Jesus, however, the other one said to Jesus; "I believe you are the Son of God. Please remember me when you are in your kingdom". Jesus did not say; "wait I have to baptize you in water first". No, Jesus said; "this day shall you be WITH me in Paradise". I am almost sure that man was NOT baptized in water before he went to Heaven. He was a criminal.

Jesus has said many times in the Bible. All you must do to get to Heaven is believe in Jesus Christ, the Son of God. The Lord is not asking anyone to build a house, make a million dollars, run a marathon, and solve a problem or anything else. ALL God is asking is for you to believe that Jesus Christ is the Son of God. God knows when you do that you will be a changed person and on your way to Heaven.

At the Last Super Jesus was with His apostles. Jesus said in St Luke 22:19-20;

"He (Jesus) took bread, and gave thanks, and brake it, and gave unto them (His apostles), saying, this is my body which is given for you. This do in remembrance of Me. (20) Likewise, also the cup after drinking, saying, this cup is the new testament in My blood, which is shed for you."

The bread was not His body. The wine was not His blood. It was an example of Him giving His body on the cross. It was an example of Him shedding His blood for all of us. Jesus said; "do this in remembrance of Me". GREATER LOVE HAS NO MAN THAN, TO LAY DOWN HIS LIFE FOR A FRIEND.

You see, the world was so evil and corrupt at the time of Jesus that it took a perfect sacrifice to shed His blood for the remission of sins. The Lord God said in the Old Testament that without the shedding of blood there is no remission of sin. Jesus was the ONE and ONLY perfect sacrifice to shed His blood to wash away ALL our sins. As you noticed earlier in this book that

there are NO more sacrifice after the sacrifice of Jesus shedding His blood on the cross.

Is it not strange to you that humanity stopped offering sacrifices after Jesus was offered as a Lamb of God for sacrifice? That is worth repeating; humanity STOPPED offering sacrifices after Jesus was offered as a Lamb of God for sacrifice.

Is it not strange to you that time as we know it started 4,000 years before Jesus, and went down to one BC and one AD when Jesus was born? Why did our calendar not start with ONE BC & AD? It is because God has a perfect plan for all of us here on earth. God has a perfect plan for TIME. Where you like it or not, God is in control. I have told you several times in this book that numbers are very important. Even today, in our lives, numbers are very important.

One of the largest religions today is followed by a man called Mohammed who was born 300 to 400 AD? Why was Mohammed not born at ONE BC & AD? However, our Lord Jesus Christ was born at ONE BC & AD. Does that not explain

something to you? Jesus is our only TRUE one and only LORD.

God even planned our calendar to fit the birth of Jesus Christ. How can any disbeliever not see our history and say Jesus is not the Son of God? Jesus is the Son of God, and I wish I could scream it from every house top and every mountain top. I know that is not possible because the evil one has blinded so many people from the truth.

As a young boy I always wondered why it was written in the Bible that Broad is the way to destruction and MANY there by that follow it. Then it says that Narrow is the way to rightness and FEW there be that find it. God is a righteous and just God. However, He has given all of us the right to choose. All of us are the ones that have made the choice to go the way we are going. That started with Adam and Eve in the Garden of Eden (Paradise) by choosing to disobey God by eating from the ONLY tree in the Garden that God said not to eat from.

Humanity has made their own choice. Do not blame God for your problems. Humanity has brought these problems upon themselves.

Often when we have a choice to choose the right or wrong way, we choose the wrong way. That is the main reason we should all pray and stay close to God. Then when a temptation is in front of us, it is so much easier to choose the right way.

ASK

I would like to write and entire chapter on this simple but needed word ASK. Webster's 1952 Dictionary says ASK is "to request; seek to obtain by WORDS, expect or require". The Bible is filled with many verses that are saying "ASK and you shall receive". Why would the Lord tell us to ASK, if He were not going to give to us what we ASK?

I will be the first one to say that I DO NOT know the way to tell you how to ASK the Lord for anything. I know how I should ASK. You will have to find out your way to ASK the Lord for what you want. You might say. "Why are you writing this, if you will not tell us how to ASK"? I am writing this because I KNOW that the Lord wants us to ASK Him when we are in need or we want something. Also, when we are praying is a good time to ASK the Lord for something. I am NOT saying ASK for money, new home, car or possessions. I am saying ANYTHING!

Am I making this clear to you?

First, the Lord is NOT our servant, so do not expect to ASK and the Lord will just give it to you. Let me

make it clear now that EVERYTHING belongs to the Lord. Therefore, all He is doing is sharing it with us. Remember that God created the earth and everything that is in and on the earth. The Lord does NOT have to share or give to you when you ASK. The Lord DOES WANT to give to you when you ASK. You are one of the many humans that God created in the beginning. He gave a choice to obey Him or go our own way. After just creating Adam and Eve, they decided to disobey Him. However, you must know that God is a loving God. The Lord protects us daily. If it were not for the Lord, ALL of us would have cancer, be in pain or even on our way to death. If God and the Holy Spirit were not with us, the evil one's goal would see to it that you are dead. Yes, many people have these diseases, and that is the only time that you ASK the Lord to help. Many doctors will admit that they do not know what happened to some of their patients, but they are healed. All I know is that through FAITH God can heal you either through doctors or simply through prayer. I do not want to give you a fake hope. Nevertheless, I have seen people with my own eyes healed through the power of God. Try it. What do you have to loss? I went to bed about an hour ago and was

praying. I could not sleep because I was praying as to how to write WORDS that would show you how to ASK. ASK with God's WORDS and receive what you want in life. I know my WORDS are not suffusion to tell you how to ASK and receive. Therefore, I was praying for the right WORDS to tell you. That is the main reason I could not sleep. So here I am on the computer again trying to express what I feel. I believed so strongly that when God said; "ask and ye shall receive". God's WORDS are a living thing! They are real. In St John 14:16 Jesus said; "I will pray the Father, and He SHALL give you another Comforter (Holy Spirit), that He may abide with you forever; (17) even the Spirit of truth". The Holy Spirit is real. The Lord's WORDS are alive. They are a living thing. Please try and grab whole to what I am trying to express to you in the early hours of this morning. Do you hear the Lord's WORDS? I am trying to tell you in a very simple way. If you could only feel what I feel now, you would see and KNOW how real God is.

Why would Jesus ASK us to Ask, if He had no intention of answering? That does not make since to me.

WORDS

Spoken WORDS have power. WORDS are a very complicated subject. First, let me mention that God created the world, as we know it, with WORDS.

St John 1:1; "In the beginning was the Word, and the Word was with God, and the Word was God. (2) The same was in the beginning with God. (3) All things were made by Him; and without Him was not anything made that was made. (4) In Him was LIFE; and the LIFE was the LIGHT of men. (5) And the light shineth in darkness; (on earth) and the darkness comprehended (understood) it not (10) He (Jesus) was in the world, and the world was made by Him, and the world knew Him not. (11) He came unto His own, and His own received Him not. (12) But as many as received Him, to them gave He the power to become the sons of God, even to them that believe on His name. (14) And the Word (Jesus) was made flesh and dwelt among us."

The SAME WORD that MADE the world.

Let all of us think for a moment—how did He create the world? He did not create it with a hammer and tools. How did God create our world as we know it today? HE CREATED IT WITH WORDS! That is incomprehensible. I DO NOT KNOW HOW HE DID IT. No one was there to witness it, but God and Lord God (Jesus).

Remember in Genesis 1:26 "And God said; let US MAKE MAN IN OUR IMAGE,

AFTER OUR LIKENESS". Moses, inspired by God, said that God created the world with WORDS, and I believe it. The Bible is the inspired WORD written, by men, but inspired by God.

Please, if you do not get anything from this writing, please understand what I just said. Ponder on it. Think about it. Do NOT be in a hurry to move on. I am trying to tell you the most important thing in this book. Please read the first paragraph about WORDS again.

Thoughtless WORDS can wound as deeply as any sword, but wisely spoken WORDS can heal.

In Webster's 1952 Dictionary the meaning of WORD is saying "an articulate sound, or combination of sounds expressing an idea". In the second meaning in Webster's WORD says; "the Son of God's Holy scripture".

We all have our meaning of WORDS. We must understand it before we can think pass this point. Even though there are hundreds of places in the Holy Bible that says 'ASK' or "speak the WORD". What does that mean? I DO NOT KNOW. However, by Faith, yes, I believe you can. Let us talk more about WORDS. We all think we know what a WORD is. Most all of us can speak WORDS. Most all of us think we know what WORDS mean. Do we? Do we really know what it means when you speak WORDS to God in prayer? Do you really know what it means when you speak WORDS to someone communicating a thought?

WORDS, WORDS and WORDS what do they mean? Some of us can communicate without WORDS. However, we are still communicating an idea or thought.

Before we leave WORDS, I want you to think about different ways of approaching WORDS. WORDS are exciting. WORDS can be used in many ways; bad or good.

Have you ever thought you could create something with WORDS? Have you ever used WORDS and they happened or came true? Have you ever used WORDS and they did not happen or come true?

Remember in the first chapter of St John where it says that Jesus was described as the "WORD"? St John could have said the Spirit, God or anything else to describe Jesus. However, he used the "WORD" to describe Jesus the Son of God and our Lord Jesus Christ. What a revelation! Why would St John do that? Was God trying to express to us how important WORDS are? Yes, He was. Our Lord was even described as "the WORD". Listen to how important WORDS are. Do you understand? Please speak out loud the reason St John described our Lord Jesus Christ as the "WORD"? I would love to hear your opinion as to the reason St John did that? Sorry, I cannot hear your answer. If I could, then

I would know what to say next. I just hope you are on the same thinking level that I am?

Speak some words sometime about what you want to happen in your life and see if they come true. Maybe I should say; "you must believe when you speak the WORDS". You cannot speak WORDS and then say to yourself "that will never happen". If it does not happen, see you were right. I feel, if you truly believe, it will happen. Maybe not the way you want it too, but God hears every WORD you say. Maybe He will give you something even better? He has given me something better than I asked for.

OBEDIENCE VS FAITH

Faith is something you MUST have in your daily life. Faith is something you MUST have in praying and dealing with the Spiritual World.

However, OBEDIANCE to God began in the very beginning with Adam and Eve. Gods placed Adam and Eve in a beautiful garden—Paradise.

Genesis 2:15 "And the Lord God took the man (Adam), and put him into the garden of Eden to dress it and to keep it. (16) And the Lord God commended the man, saying, of every tree of the garden thou mayest freely eat; (17) But of the tree of the knowledge of good and evil, thou shalt NOT eat of it: for the day that thou eat thereof thou shalt surely die".

Then God made Eve from one of Adam's ribs.

Genesis 3:2 "And the woman (Eve) said unto the serpent. We may eat of the fruit of the trees of the garden: (3) But of the fruit from the tree which is in the midst of the garden, God hath said, ye shall NOT eat of it, neither shall ye touch it, lest ye die. (4) And the serpent said unto the

women, ye shall not surely die. (5) For God doth know that in the day ye eat thereof, then your eyes shall be opened, and ye shall be as gods, knowing good from evil".

Adam and Eve DISOBEDIANCE to God. THAT WAS THEIR SIN UNTO GOD. God does not ask hard things of us, but the things God ask He wants us to OBEY. God said DO NOT EAT from the "tree of knowledge of good and evil". Adam and Eve had everything in Paradise. Why did they DISOBEY God? Why do we DISOBEY God? God has taught us in His Bible how to eat, sleep, exercise and even how to pray, and yet we DISOBEY. WHY?

Yes, Adam and Eve's eyes were opened, and they realized they were naked. Yes, in the day they ate of the fruit they died. Would Adam and Eve have lived FOREVER, if they did not DISOBEY God? I do not know.

Remember me telling you earlier that the Bible says, "a Day in the site of God is as a thousand years, and a thousand years as a Day (II Peter 3:28)?" All the people before Noah did NOT live over a thousand years. Noah's grandfather

lived 969 years, then died the year of the flood. According to the Bible, up to the day of Noah, men's minds and actions were very evil. Then God destroyed the people living on earth, at that time, with water. All of them. ONLY Noah and his family survived. Life started over again for humans. This time God only promised man a hundred years. Yes, a few people live more than 100 years. I am sure there is a good reason behind it.

FAITH with BELIEVING

As I have mentioned earlier in this book, FAITH is something you must believe and accept. FAITH is a vehicle stronger than any other for you to receive what you want. Faith is something you need to visualize and crystalize in your mind until you receive it. Maybe I should say that you need to practice with FAITH for a while until you get it right. I will write about DOUBT next. How can I express to you? When you visualize and crystalize anything in your mind that is the beginning of FAITH. FAITH and BELIEVING work hand in hand to get you what you are desiring.

Jesus was walking through a crowd one time, and He said someone has touched me. His disciples said Lord many people have touched you. Then Jesus said in St Luke 8:46 to 48 says:

(46) And Jesus said, someone hath touched Me: for I perceive that virtue is gone out of Me. (47) And when the woman saw that she was not hid, she came trembling, and, falling down before Him, she declared unto Him before all the people for what reason she had touched Him, and how she was healed immediately. (48) And He said

unto her, daughter, be of good comfort: YOUR FAITH HATH MADE YOU WHOLE; go in peace.

Notice Jesus said: HER FAITH HAD MADE HER WHOLE. It was NOT Jesus' FAITH. It was her FAITH. Another example is St Matthew 21:21 & 22 says:

(21) "Jesus answered and said unto them, verily I say unto you, if you have FAITH, and DOUBT not, you shall say unto this mountain, be thou removed, and be thou cast into the sea: it shall be done. (22) And all things, whatsoever you shall ask in prayer, believing, you shall receive."

I will write more about DOUBT shortly. St Matthew 17:20 "Jesus said unto them, because of your unbelief: for verily I say unto you, if you have FAITH as a grain of mustard seed, you shall say unto this mountain; 'remove hence to another place', and it shall be removed; and nothing shall be impossible unto you."

Jesus was comparing your FAITH even to the size of a mustard seed. A Mustard seed is the smallest seed we know of on earth. Do you understand that Jesus was telling us even with

the smallest amount of FAITH "nothing shall be impossible unto you?" Just STOP for a minute and think about that. You can work miracles with, just a little FAITH. That is more than I can understand. I still BELIEVE every word in the Bible. All I can say is; "just believe it".

DOUBT

Just think of some of the greatest men in the Bible. After John the Baptist had baptized Jesus, the Spirit of God ascended on Him and remained there. John said, "Behold the Lamb of God that taketh away the sins of the world." John knew Jesus was the Christ. However, after he was placed in prison, John asked two of his Disciples to go to Jesus and ask, "If He is the Christ, or should we search for another?" That does not mean John was weak. My opinion was John admitting he was human and wanted to reassure himself if what he BELIEVED was true. It is alright to have DOUBT like this.

Little king David BELIEVED and had FAITH that he could kill the giant. Then he did it. David knew God would help him with what he needed to do. David goes down to the brook/creek and got five (5) smooth stones. All David needed was one stone. Somehow a little DOUBT arose. If he did not kill the giant with one stone, he would have four more to kill him. Like David with the FIVE stones to kill Goliath of Gath. All he needed was ONE, however, he wanted to

be sure. David knew his God, and the God of Israel, would help him kill this giant. DOUBT like this is alright. Yes, this is the same David that became the second King of all of Israel. (II Samuel 5:3) "All the elders of Israel came to the king to Hebron; and king David made a league with them in Hebron before the Lord; and they anointed David king over Israel." Like in St Matthew 21:21 in the previous verse, Jesus said: "to have FAITH and DOUBT not". That is a deferent DOUBT. I hope you see the difference? There are many examples in the Bible about FAITH 101 and DOUBT.

KNOW

Do you KNOW God loves you? Do you KNOW the Lord wants you to have your heart's desire? Do you KNOW the Holy Spirit wants to comfort you? In your need and ALL the time. There are a lot of things in our life we would like to KNOW. There are a lot of things in life we will never KNOW. We need to KNOW God loves us! Do you? I KNOW God loves me!

When Jesus had the prayer of Intercession before His crucifixion He said:

"(3) And this is life eternal, that they might KNOW Thee the only TRUE God, and Jesus Christ, whom thou hast sent. (4) I have glorified Thee on the earth: I have finished the work which Thou gave Me to do. (5) And now, O Father, glorify Thou Me with Thine own Self with the glory which I HAD WITH THEE BEFORE THE WORLD WAS." St John 17:3-5

Is there ANY way I can make this more clear?

That is worth repeating: "The glory I (Jesus) had with Thee (God) before the world was". Sorry

to change the subject, but earlier in this book I was trying to tell you that Jesus was with God when they created Adam and Eve. Jesus even said it in His prayer.

When there is something you do not understand, start you a folder or file intitled "I do not understand". Lock it up and forget it. Someday the Holy Spirit will reveal it to you. When there is a PERIOD, do not put a QUESTION MARK. There are many things in life I do not understand. There will be many things in your life also. Do not try and create something just so you can say; "I know that". In our front car window is a large glass to look forward. A small mirror to look back. Looking forward is much more important than looking back. If you do not understand, lock it in your "I do not understand" folder. File it and keep looking forward to your dream. The story is told of a young man going to the airport and had a flat tire. He missed his flight. His plane was the one that ran into the twin towers on 9/11. Months later a lady showed up at his door with a baby in her arms. She told the young man that she

named the baby after his father who saved her life from the fire on 9/11. Keep looking forward.

There are things in our life that we do not understand. Accept it and move on.

We must control our minds. I have had trouble most of my life thinking about good Godly things and not bad things. God's Spirit will help us to control our minds. I am much better now after years of training my mind.

You might wonder why I refer to a book, called the Bible, so many times. It is a book that was written thousands of years ago. However, the truths that are written in the Bible do apply to our fast moving, technologically advanced world. Many people think the Bible is for theologians. NO! The Bible is for you and me in this day and time in our life.

There are many parts of the Bible that have amazed me. For instance, when King David was writing the 23rd Psalm: "The Lord is my Shepherd. I shall not want (2) He makes me to lie down in green pastures; He leadeth me beside the still waters (3) He restoreth my soul: He leadeth me

in the paths of righteousness for His name's sake…" When you read the entire 23rd chapter, you can see the closeness he had with the Lord. Why does this seem so strange to me? Do you realize this was written approximately 1500 to 2000 years before Jesus came to earth as a real Human Being? The only way David could know so much about the Lord was what the prophets had said, before Him. David had an experience with the Lord that was very special. David did not have to know for sure Jesus was coming to earth. He did not have to see or witness people seeing Jesus in his past. David believed that Jesus was coming and, therefore, he KNEW in his heart that Jesus is REAL.

David called Jesus his Shepherd—his Savior. David felt, in his heart, "Lord (Jesus) MAKETH me to lie down in green pastures". Not the desert, but a soft, fertile, green grassy land to rest. "He (Lord) leadeth me beside the still waters". I picture this as deep calm waters. "Jesus (Lord) restored my soul". That was the MOST important part of David's being. "Jesus (Lord) leadeth me in the paths of righteousness

for His name's sake". Can you NOT feel how close David was to the Lord? I can feel it.

It is easy for me to see Jesus' disciples get close to Him. They could see, touch and hear Jesus. However, David lived about 1500 to 2000 years before Jesus came to earth. Blessed is the man who trust and believe in Jesus and have NEVER seen, heard or touched Him. Think about this. Have you seen, heard or touched Jesus? Can you still believe and trust Jesus? David did. I feel we have an advantage over David because we KNOW Jesus did come to earth as a Human Being.

By faith, we can feel Jesus. We can see Him with our spiritual eyes. We can know He is REAL even though we have never seen, heard or touched Him. That is REAL faith. Can you believe in Jesus even though you have never seen, heard or touched Him? I can, and I do.

Again, I say, if I have said anything in this book to cause you to want to study the Bible more, I have completed what I wanted to do.

Love God and Jesus. Then study His Bible to know Him more. To love Him more. To thank Him for dying for you and me. Stop and think for a moment what Jesus did by shedding His blood on the cross for ours sins—NOT His. We should be thinking Him every moment for the rest of our lives.

WHY DO WE
CLOSE OUR EYES
WHEN WE PRAY
CRY, KISS OR DREAM? IT IS BECAUSE THE
MOST BEAUTIFUL
THINGS IN OUR LIFE ARE NOT SEEN
BUT FELT BY OUR HEART ONLY!

Study your Bible.

God will take care of you…

Throughout our lives we have heard from our parents, teachers, ministers and all other people that seem to be over us. As a child, remember them saying; "do not do that", "NO", "that is not right", "stop" and a lot of other negative comments.

Now you are grown you need to start thinking, I can do that", "YES", "that is right", "do it", and a lot of other positive comments. Do not say "no, I cannot". Say "yes, I can". Change your thinking to be positive. God, the Lord Jesus Christ and the Holy Spirit CAN DO ANYTHING! We are the sons and daughters of God. We need to start acting like it.

WHEN YOU FACE A DEAD END, DO NOT FOCUS ON WHAT YOU CANNOT DO. FOCUS INSTEAD ON WHAT GOD CAN DO!

Luke 18:27 "And Jesus said, the things which are impossible with man are possible with God".

What am I trying to say? DO NOT be conditioned by all the things you have heard. Also, the things that have happened to you in your childhood and all through your life. Wake up! All things are possible! NO, you cannot do all things, but, if God is with you, ALL THINGS ARE POSSIBLE!

I just got through watching the movie; The Count of Monte Cristo (latest edition). When he was placed in prison wrongfully, he saw written on the wall "God will take care of you". After many years of losing faith that he would ever get out, he even said; "I do not believe in God now". Then seemingly from nowhere, a priest dug his way into his cell. To make a long story shorter, he broke out of prison. Before the priest died, he gave him a map telling him where the treasure of the Count of Monte Cristo was located. His life was changed. However, the priest told him NOT to use the money for revenge. He did. The end of his life was greater than it had ever been.

That is the way we must think about life. Look for something GOOD to happen in your life. Expect great things for the future of your life. Let your mind reach out and draw good things

to you. Allow God to do special things in your life. From now forward—think positive. All these things could happen any time. Expect them. Receive them. Know that they are on the way to you.

Every morning I wake up, two miracles happen to me. I open my two eyes that I can see. Can I get you to expect a miracle every morning you wake up? How can I get you to expect good things in your life? How can I get you to have faith in our creator? How can I unlock the sleeping giant of faith in you? My wish is I were there with you to express how I feel here and now... God is REAL.

One of my goals in life is to come into a large sum of money before passing on to Heaven. I would love to travel everywhere finding REALLY NEEDY people and give the money to them. I do not mean people that waste money. I mean real people that need money to survive. Yes, I believe God will let me do this someday.

When I was a teenager, I wrote a lot of my goals on paper. I would repeat them every day and believe they are really going to happen. I guess

my life has taken a lot of turns that I did not plan. That is the reason you must believe that someday they will happen in your life. It does not matter what comes or goes. You must keep believing. That is the reason every morning I get up I am wondering if this is the day. My goal will take place when God is ready to give it to me. I cannot reach my goal by myself. There must be a divine intervention from God for me to reach my goal.

Our brain is like a machine. If you keep telling yourself a lie, you will start believing it is the truth. The same way you keep repeating something that is going to happen in your life. It will happen. Believe me it will happen.

Program your mind to believe something good will happen. It will happen. Say it. Believe it. Trust me it will happen. I do not know when, but it will happen. God's universe and Spirit will cause it to happen. I dare you to try it. Just dare to believe that it will happen. YOU MUST BELIEVE. All things in life are trying to work together for the good of our lives and for our universe. Believe me.

I have not finished talking about our brain. I said it was like a machine. However, the deference in our brain and a machine is God created our brain. Man created a machine. There is a big deference. Being God has created our brain, we can tap into God's universe. We can communicate directly with God through Jesus Christ and the Holy Spirit. Why do we not do that? We just do NOT believe we can. We have been conditioned, our whole life, we cannot. Break away from what you have been taught. NOW is the time to change the way you think. Now is the time to reach out to the unlimited belief in God. NOW is the time to tap into God's universe. NOW is the time to say: "I can". NOW is the time to believe you can. Do it. I dare you!

COMMITMENT

Think about it for a few moments. Everything in our human life, that is good, we should COMMIT—for example; marriage, job, school, learning, friends in our lives and many other things.

Marriage—we should be faithful. We should love him or her, with all the love we have. Love with everything. Always give everything, that we are capable of giving. With all the love we know. That means being nice, complimenting them as much as possible. Be faithful—do not flirt with someone else. Commit your mind and soul to the marriage.

Job—we should work hard and smart every day at our job. Do not steal items, time or ideas from your work. Make your job pleasant.

School—we should always be on time. Listen to the teacher to really learn. Trust me, some day you will need it.

Learn—we should always try to learn throughout our lives. I mean with everything, and every part of your life.

Friends—we should use the "Golden Rule", do unto others as you would have them do unto you. You should respect and love your friends. Even the Apostle Paul that wrote more books in the New Testament than anyone else said, that he wants all of us to make sure that we love everyone.

Just think of all the Apostles that made a COMMITMENT to Jesus. All of them were put to death because they refused to denounce Jesus. That is except St John. Jesus would not allow John to die until a very old age. He died after writing the last book in the Bible called Revelations.

The only way you will be successful in life is to COMMIT to the things that are right, and the things you care about. COMMITING is not something very hard to do. You MUST "kiss the past good by". Live for the future.

Did you ever think of how much of a COMMITMENT Jesus made to come to earth for all of us? That is proven to us in the first chapter of Genesis. For approximately four thousand years no one had seen or talked to God. God did send Angels to earth during that four thousand years to meet and talk with us. In the beginning God did create Heaven and Earth. Then we notice in;

GENESIS 1:26 "God said, let US make man in OUR image, after OUR likeness; and let them have dominion over…EVERYTHING". (27) So, God created man in HIS own image".

Who do you think God was talking to, when He said; "let US make man in OUR image, after OUR likeness"? Do you think someone else was there? God was not talking to Adam, because he had not created him yet.

Let us go to Genesis 2:4 & 7;

"These are the generations of the Heavens and the Earth when they were created, in the day that the LORD GOD made the Earth and the Heavens. (7) And the LORD GOD formed man

of the dust of the ground and breathed into his (Adam) nostrils the breath of LIFE; and man became a living soul." Jesus was referred to as LORD, though out the Bible. When Earth was created, Jesus had not been born yet. Who was US in Genesis 1:26? It was GOD and LORD GOD. How do you refer to GOD's SON, other than as LORD GOD? Please stop and think about this for a moment……………………………………

Remember, earlier in this book I quoted from St John1:1,2,3 & 14; "In the beginning was the WORD and the WORD was with GOD, and the WORD was GOD…without HIM was not anything made that was made…in HIM was LIFE; and the LIFE was the LIGHT of men…and the WORD was made FLASH, and dwelt among us". Back to Genesis 2:4 "…breathed into Adam's nostrils the breath of LIFE, Adam became a living soul."

How much more do we need to see that LORD (Jesus) God was with God. I know it is hard for many of you to accept this. Think about it for a moment. You must see this. Open your eyes. Think outside the box.

We all must accept God the Father, Lord Jesus Christ and the Holy Spirit by faith. Jesus Christ was COMMITTED and kind enough to leave His Heavenly home. Jesus came to earth as one of us. Jesus lived like one of us. Jesus would eat, slept and was tempted like one of us. Jesus had pain like one of us. Why? Why did Jesus come to earth and live like one of us? God wrote in the law without the shedding of blood there is no redemption of sin. Jesus was the ONLY spotless sacrifice to offer for our sins. Jesus would bleed like one of us. Therefore, Jesus shed His blood for our sins. All of it. By doing that, we could be saved and go to Heaven to be with God and Jesus.

All Jesus asked of us is that we believe He is the Son of God, and the Savior of the world. We do not have to wait for the Messier to come. Jesus has ALREADY come. Jesus has already died for our sins. In the Bible it says; "with His (Jesus) strips we WERE healed". NOW all we must do is believe on Jesus. Yes, Jesus is coming again.

Jesus (God's Son) lived approximately 2,000 years ago on this earth. Jesus is now in a spiritual

world with God the Father. Jesus is God the Son. Yes, Jesus is coming to earth again. No, we do not know when. Jesus will come again in the East. That is where He ascended to Heaven to be with God.

Moses, David and all the Holy men and women in the Old Testament really did need to have faith that God existed. It should be easier for us to believe, because Jesus was born before us, and, yes, He lived here on earth like one of us. We have records like the Bible and other books telling Jesus lived and worked miracles here on earth. Jesus taught us how to love one another. He taught us how to believe in God (St John 3:16). He taught us how to pray to God (St Luke 11:2 to 4). He taught us how to believe in Jesus as our Christ/Savior and Messiah and be saved by Jesus. THESE ARE JUST A FEW REASONS JESUS CAME TO EARTH.

Well, I would like to talk about this more. Jesus is the Son of God. Jesus is the one and only Son of God on earth where we could see, touch, and hear His voice. Jesus is not an idol. Jesus Christ came to earth to shed His blood and die for you

and me. Jesus was the only perfect sacrifice to come to earth and shed His blood for you and me.

In the beginning God said; "without the shedding of blood there is no remission of sin". For 4,000 years holy people offered lambs, birds, and all types of animals that were the best of what they owned. I mean the ones without being sick. I mean the ones without a spot. I mean the perfect ones they owned. When it came the change from the law of Moses to the law of Love with Jesus, God had to have a sinless, perfect, unquestionable sacrifice to offer. The shedding of blood for the remission of sins—all sins. There could ONLY be One—Jesus Christ. Yes, Jesus felt pain. Yes, Jesus shed His blood. However as predicted thousands of years before His death, NOT one bone in His Body was broken. Usually before one of their Sabbath days that week begin at six PM, the soldiers would go around and break the legs of the ones on the cross. That is if they were not already dead. However, when they came to Jesus, they said He was already dead. Therefore, the soldiers thrust a spear in His side to let Him

shed all His blood. As the Prophies for 4,000 years said, "not one bone of His Body shall be broken".

Have you ever wondered how Jesus was seen many times, for 40 days after His death? Some people even touched Him. No one said; "Jesus, you feel cold". He had a new body. How can that be? How can Jesus have a new living, breathing body? Even after He was completely dead? Have you ever wondered about that? If we died and do not come back, after a reasonable time, we are dead. Our body starts decaying, drying up and returning to a substance like the earth. Jesus was dead in the tomb for three days and returned with a new body. You might say; "He was not completely dead?" That would not be true. Jesus died on the cross, and then the soldiers truss a spear into His side, so He would lose the rest of the blood that might be in His body. Yes, He died. Jesus died for you and me. Jesus died to fulfill prophesies for about 4,000 years before Him in the Old Testament. Yes, Jesus was completely dead.

I do not truly know what Jesus did while He was dead in the tomb for three days. However, implied in the Bible, He entered Hell. There Jesus proved to the devil that He (Jesus) was King of ALL. He is King forever in the future. We know He was the King in the beginning, and He will be the King forever.

We KNOW our beginning. We DO NOT KNOW all things in the middle term of our lives we have not endured. We have faith for things we have asked God for in our future. By faith I KNOW the end of my life. However, I do NOT KNOW the things I must go through to get to the end of my life. Though I do NOT KNOW the things ahead, I feel God will help me all the way to the end.

It is April 17, 2019 at 11:20 PM and I just got a Bone MRI to see if I have bone cancer. I had a kidney bio on May 10, 2019 at Boca Raton Hospital. I had to stay in bed for 24 hours. I was fine from that. However, on May 20, 2019 I went back to my cancer specialist doctor, and she wants me to start chemo ASAP. Then she wants me to see a heart doctor and some other doctors. Then

she wants me to start taking chemo May 24th. I will deal with whatever life throws at me. I really feel God will heal me. Thank you, Jesus.

With Jesus' help it will NOT be as serious as the doctor is saying. I feel it is the Lord's will to heal me. Jesus has not let me live to old age then let me go like this. I believe in the total power of our Lord Jesus Christ. With the stripes of Jesus, I am healed. However, with God's help, I am ready for whatever happens.

With that, being said, how does a person act with a secret aliment in you? The aliment is trying to destroy your life. You know in your heart and mind that God can heal you and destroy ANY sickness. Jesus did so many times when He was here on earth. Jesus said in St John 14:12; "I say unto you, he that believeth on Me, the works that I do shall he do also; and greater works than these shall he do; because I go unto My Father." Then in Luke 9:1; "power was given to His disciples to cure the sick". I am sure that means that we MUST have faith to destroy this secret aliment. We MUST believe in Jesus, then let Him get rid of this secret

aliment. Lord help me to believe. Lord also get rid of any doubt I may have. Also NEVER give up to what the devil has in mind for you or me. God can and will heal you or me. I BELIEVE IT! I really, really believe it.

**KEEP WALKING THROUGH THE STORM.
YOUR EAINBOW IS WAITING
ON THE OTHER SIDE.**

Please pray that ALL the world's diseases may be healed. God, please help all of us that might have a disease. Thank You, Jesus...

Always remember; TRY TO DIE YOUNG IN OLD AGE.

Jesus had His beginning, middle and future prophesied in the Bible. We know He was in the beginning. We know about His birth. We do not know but one thing Jesus did during the first 30 years of His life. We know a lot about the three main years of His life and ministry. We know He is forever. We do not know all the things He did while on earth as a human being. Jesus let us know the things He wanted us to know. That is all. I feel if EVERYTHING Jesus did was written down that all the libraries of this world could be filled with just the life of Him. Jesus is more than any of us can comprehend. Do you realize Jesus was/is God in a human body? Jesus had the wisdom of God. It is more than I can ever understand that God would send His Son

to earth to be a human like us. Jesus dwelt with us and taught us the right way of God almighty. Jesus was NOT an idol. Jesus was NOT just a human being placed here on His earth. Jesus was God's Son. The Jews are looking for the Messiah, the Holy One to come someday. I have news for them and you. Jesus has already come to this world. However, Jesus will come again as He told us.

Jesus prayed to God to send us another Comforter (Holy Spirit). Jesus wants the Holy Spirit to be with us until Jesus returns someday. How can this NOT be so clear to everyone? Jesus said: "I will pray the Father and He shall give you Another Comforter that He MAY abide with you for ever (two words to emphasize); even the Spirit of truth, whom the world cannot receive because they see Him not". St John 14:16 & 17.

When Jesus was having the Passover meal with His disciples, He said; St John 14:1

"Let not you heart be troubled: ye believe in God, believe also in Me. (2) In My Father's house are many mansions: if it were not so, I would have told you. I go to prepare a place for you.

(3) And if I go and prepare a place for you, I will come again, and receive you unto myself; that where I am, there ye may be also. (4) And whither I go ye know, and the way ye know."

Then Thomas had to speak up and say;

"5) Thomas said unto Him, Lord, we know not whither thou go; and how can we know the way? (6) Jesus said unto him, I am the WAY, the TRUTH, and the LIFE: NO MAN COMETH UNTO the Father, BUT BY ME."

Remember, earlier I said that St John described Jesus as the Word. How can you NOT believe the Word (Jesus) helped God to create Adam? St John 1:4;

"In Him (Jesus) was LIFE; and the LIFE was the Light of men." This is the SAME LIFE that was breathed into Adam and Eve.

St John was saying Jesus was describing "ETERNAL LIFE". St John inspired by God to write in Revelation 22:19;

"If any man shall take away from the WORDS of the Book of this prophecy, God shall take away

his part out of the book of LIFE, and out of the Holy City, and from the things which are written in the Book."

When people say they cannot understand the Bible. What they are really saying is they do not BELIEVE the Bible. If the Bible says something— anything, believe it. The Bible is not just a lot of stories. It is the TRUTH! When the Bible says something, you can believe it. Do not try and analyze it. Just believe what it says.

Let me make clear SOME of the things in the Bible are prophecies of our FUTURE. ONE THIRD of the Bible is prophecy. For example; the book of Revelation is mainly a prophecy of Jesus Christ which is, and which was, and which are things to come. Yes, St John uses symbols and things to represent other things. Once you know what those symbols and things are, you need to believe them and to know they are TRUTH. (I shall write a book on Revelation later).

CLOSE THE DOOR TO YOUR PAST.

OPEN THE DOOR TO YOUR FUTURE.

TAKE A DEEP BREATH, AND

STEP THROUGH TO A NEW LIFE.

There was a man crucified on each side of Jesus. One went to Heaven the other one probable did not. Let us look at St Luke 23:41,42,43

"And we indeed justly; for we receive the due reward of our deeds; but this man (Jesus) hath done nothing amiss. (42) And he said unto Jesus, Lord remember me when thou cometh into thy kingdom. (43) And Jesus said unto him, 'Verily I say unto thee; today shalt thou be with Me in Paradise'."

Look and see where I wrote more about this earlier?

Many things in our everyday lives, I do not understand. For instance, our day starts at midnight. It is still dark, and our day starts at MIDNIGHT. It is still dark, but we KNOW the light will come. Sometimes when I get depressed, I think this is a new day, and the light will come. You MUST believe that. Remember in the first chapter of St John, Jesus is LIFE and the LIFE

was and is the LIGHT of the world. This is what I think about when I get out of bed in the middle of the night. I walk through the condo, or I set down at the computer and write. I pray through the Holy Spirit for the LIGHT from the LIFE of Jesus Christ, and I know the LIGHT will come—just like daylight. I just had to put this thought in this book.

Remember, God has PROMISED us many things. God is not a man that He should lie. Numbers 23:19 says;

"God is not a man, that He should lie; neither the son of man, that He should repent: hath He said, and shall He not do it? Or hath He spoken, and shall He not make it good?"

God PROMISED Abraham his seed would be many. Genesis 13:16 says;

"I (Lord) will make thy seed as the dust of the earth; so that if a man can number the dust of the earth, then shall thy seed also be numbered."

God PROMISED that we would Lien and not Borrow. Deuteronomy 15:6 says;

"For the Lord thy God shall bless thee, as He promised thee; and thou shalt LEND unto many nations, but thou shalt not BORROW." Also in Deuteronomy 28:12 says; "The Lord shall open unto thee His good treasure, and the Heaven to give the rain unto thy land in his season, and to bless all the work of thine hand; and thou shalt LEND unto many nations, and thou shalt not BORROW."

This book is NOT about me. However, when President Obama was in office in 2014, I was worth over two million dollars. In 2015 my net worth was zero. I wish I could have held on until President Trump had gotten in office. I would have been living on the beach, instead of five miles from the beach. President Obama's economy wrecked the United States for eight years. The US went from 8 ½ trillion to 18 ½ trillion. What a shame. Sorry, but I just had to say that.

God PROMISED King David his relatives would be on the throne of Israel for many years in the future. From David to Hezekiah was 305 years. David son Solomon did wrong and his son did

not set on his throne. Then Hezekiah's son became king when Hezekiah died. Manasseh was twelve years old. He reigned for 55 years in Jerusalem. Manasseh sinned by rebuilding the altars to worship Baal and many other sinful things. The Lord God said in II Kings 21;

"(7) to David, and to Solomon his son, in this house, and in Jerusalem, which I chosen out of all tribes of Israel, will I put my name for ever. (8) Neither will I make the feet of Israel move any more out of the land which I gave their fathers; only if they will observe to do according to all that I have commanded them, and according to all the law that my servant Moses commanded them. (9) But they hearkened not: and Manasseh, seduced them to do more evil, than did the nations whom the Lord destroyed before the children of Israel. (11) Because Manasseh king of Judah hath done these abominations, and that done wickedly above all that the Amorites did, which were before him, and hath made Judah also to sin with his idols. (12) Therefore, thus saith the Lord God of Israel, behold, I will bring such evil upon Jerusalem and Judah, that

whosoever heareth of it, both his ears shall tingle.

I had to tell this story, because the Lord God loved David so much. That is the reason God promised David that he or his house shall reign on the throne of Israel for many years in the future. When we love God like David did. God will promise many blessings. I am trying to say God is not like LOVE, He is LOVE. Thank about that for a moment. God is LOVE. Where do you think we get our LOVE? We get it from God. Yes, we get it from God. As I said earlier in this book, I will write more about LOVE at the end of this book. I will call it, "The Circle of LOVE".

God has used imperfect people in imperfect situations to get His will done.

Excuses: Moses said; "I can't talk". Gideon said; "I'm too young". Abraham said; "I'm too old". What is your excuse?

What is the will of the Lord for us? Ephesians 5:15 to 18;

"See then, that ye walk circumspectly, not as fools, but as wise. (16) redeeming the time, because the days are evil. (17) Wherefore, be ye not unwise, but understanding what the will of the Lord is. (18) Be not drunk with wine, wherein is excess; but be filled with the Spirit (Holy Spirit)."

All of us need WISDOM from God. Let us look in James 3:17 that says;

"The Wisdom that is from above is first pure, then peaceable, gentle, and easy to be interested, full of mercy and good fruits, without partiality, and without hypocrisy."

In St Luke 2:41 to 52 says;

(42) "When Jesus was twelve years old, they went up to Jerusalem after the custom of the feast. (43) And when they had fulfilled the days, as they returned, the child Jesus tarried behind in Jerusalem; and Joseph and Mary knew not of it. (45) And when they found Him not, they turned back again to Jerusalem. (46) And it came to pass, that after three days they found Jesus in the temple, setting in the middle of the

doctors, both hearing them, and asking them questions. (47) And all that heard Him were astonished at His understanding and answers. (49) And Jesus said unto them, how is it that you sought me? Did ye not know that I must be about my Father's business? (52) And Jesus increased in WISDOM and stature, and in favor with God and man."

Remember, "God is a Spirit; and they that worship Him must worship Him in Spirit and in truth." St John 4:24, Jesus, now, lives in the Spirit? The Holy Spirit is a Spirit. Therefore, we should worship God, Jesus and the Holy Spirit in the Spirit. St John 16:16-17;

"And I (Jesus) will pray the Father, and He shall give you another Comforter, that He may abide with you forever: (17) Even the Spirit of Truth…".

If you have never learned how to pray in the Spirit, you need to learn. Do not be afraid to ask the Lord for anything and expect to receive it. Yes, I said anything!

Let me pray with you NOW. You should be able to ask God, in the name of Jesus for anything.

Yes, I said anything. God in the name of Jesus through the Holy Spirit will you GIVE this person what they are praying for. Lord, you told us in your Bible that; "whatsoever we shall ask in My (Jesus) name, I (Jesus) will do it". I do not know who is, reading this book, or praying NOW. All I know is You (Jesus), said You (Jesus) "WOULD DO IT". Thank you, Jesus for answering this prayer.

If you are still reading this book, I am proud of you. I need to leave a few more thoughts with you.

Have you read the Bible? A lot? If so, please tell me of just one place in the Bible that Jesus did NOT heal any and ALL people that came to Him and asked Jesus for healing? There are none. Jesus healed ALL that came to Him, and even some that did not come to Him. Did you hear what I just said? Jesus HEALED ALL, and ALL type diseases. I need to say that again. Jesus HEALED ALL the people. ALL. Jesus also raised the DEAD and caused them to live again. Can I make this, even clearer? Jesus is LIFE. Read again; "Jesus is LIFE". You must see what I am

seeing. I would love to think I have convinced you by now that; "Jesus is LIFE"?

St John 14:6; "Jesus said unto His apostles, I am the Way, the Truth, and the LIFE: no man cometh unto the Father, but by Me".

St Matthew 4:23; "Jesus went about all Galilee, teaching in their synagogues, and preaching the gospel of the kingdom, and HEALING ALL manner of sickness and ALL manner of disease among the people".

St Matthews 15:29; "And Jesus departed from then and came nigh unto the sea of Galilee: and went up into a mountain and sat there. (30) And great multitudes came unto Him, having with them those that were lame, blind and dumb, maimed and many others, cast them down at Jesus' feet; and He healed them. (31) Insomuch that the multitudes wondered, when they saw the dumb to speak, and the maimed to be whole, the lame to walk, and the blind to see, and they glorified the God of Israel."

We know that Jesus Healed ALL the sick that asked. He also raised the dead. As I said before,

do you know of ONE person that came to Jesus and, He did NOT heal them? I do NOT. Jesus loves you, me and everyone. He wants us to be well. He wants us to be healed. He wants us to follow Him. He wants ALL of us to be in Paradise with Him. God the Father is the same way.

St John 3:16 "For God so loved the world..." That includes ALL--you and me.

However, Jesus also gave power to His twelve disciples to heal the sick.

St Matthew 10:1; "When He (Jesus) had called unto Him (Jesus) His twelve disciples, He gave them power against unclean spirits, to cast them out, and to heal ALL manner of sickness and ALL manner of disease."

The Acts 5:15; "Insomuch that they brought forth the sick into the streets, and laid them on beds and couches, that at the least the shadow of Peter passing by might overshadow some of them. (16) There came also a multitude out of the cities round about unto Jerusalem, bringing sick folks, and them which were vexed with unclean spirits: and they were healed EVERYONE."

Proverbs 16:24; "Pleasant words are as a honeycomb, sweet to the SOUL, and health to the BONES". I felt I needed to insert this here, because I have someone very close that is going to need a Bone Transplant.

Positive or Negative—Jesus went to a little girl's home to heal her or bring her back to life? Jesus told all the people to leave except Peter and John because of their unbelief. You MUST be Positive and not Negative. Jesus knew the people were Negative, so He asked them to leave. You MUST be Positive even now, when you ask for healing from our Lord Jesus Christ.

BE POSITIVE WHEN YOU PRAY.

1 Peter 2:24; "Who His (Jesus) Own Self bare our sins in His Own Body on the tree, that we, being dead to sins, should live unto righteousness: BY WHOSE STRIPES YE WERE HEALED".

We are already healed. All we must do is ACCEPT it. Are you reading what I am saying? Are you believing what I am saying? If not? Why not? Did you read what I just quoted; "Who His Own Self bare our SINS in His Own Body on the tree". I know you were thinking you needed to get rede of your sins first. Can you NOT see that Jesus bare OUR sins in His Own Body on the tree? Forgive yourself and believe in Jesus Christ. Oh, if we could only believe this. Jesus LOVES us so much that He died for us. He shed all His blood for our SINS and sickness. If only, you could believe that with your mind and heart. Maybe then we could find a way for us to be healed and our sins forgiven. I do not know the reason you are reading this book. However, if Jesus tells us something—anything, we MUST believe it. We MUST accept it. We MUST not doubt it. Try it. See if it works. Trust me, it works. I need

to say more about this before I go forward to something else.

Sometimes I wonder if I am writing this book for you or me? Because the more I write the more I believe that ALL of this is TRUTH and REAL. You must believe it also. If not, I wished you could tell me what is on your mind—at this moment? Being you cannot, I will press on and try everything I can to get you to believe everything I am believing NOW.

Say, "I CAN" do not say "I CANNOT".

There are plenty of rich people that love God and are going to Heaven. However, a very rich man came to Jesus and ask; "what shall I do to inherit eternal life?" Jesus saw that he was very rich. Jesus also knew the man's riches is what he worshiped. Therefore, Jesus told him to sale all he had and give it to the poor. The man left very sorrowful. Jesus said; "it is easier for a camel to go through a needle's eye, than for a rich man to enter into the kingdom of God". A lot of people would then say, how can a rich man enter Heaven? A needle's eye is a arched gate before you enter a property. The only way

a camel can enter the yard is to get down on its knees and crawl in. A camel does not like to be cold. If a camel can find a warm place, it will stick its nose in a tent or home. They did not have needles then the way we have them today.

There are so many things in the Bible that are misunderstood.

Read and study your Bible.

"LORD JESUS CHRIST"

JESUS, JESUS, JESUS, JESUS, JESUS, JESUS, JESUS, JESUS, JESUS, JESUS, JESUS...

THIS IS THE MOST MOMENTOUS UNIQUE IMPORTANT CHAPTER IN THIS BOOK.

I really cannot describe who Jesus was and is. I can only get you to read how Jesus and others describe Jesus.

Mary, the mother of Jesus, tells us the first story in St Luke 1:31: "Behold, you shall conceive in thy womb, and bring forth a Son, and shall call His name JESUS. (34) Then said Mary unto the Angel, how shall this be, seeing I know NOT

a man? (35) And the Angel answered and said unto her (Mary). The Holy Spirit (said) shall come upon thee, and the Power of the Highest shall overshadow thee; therefore, also that Holy Thing which shall be born of thee shall be called the Son of God. (37) For with God nothing shall be impossible." (Jesus was NOT the Son of Joseph)—JESUS WAS NOT THE SON OF JOSEPH!

St John 14:6 Jesus (said); "I Am the Way, the Truth, and the Life: no man cometh unto the Father, but by Me." Then Jesus said:

St John 3:16; "For God (said) so LOVED the world, that He gave His ONLY BEGOTTEN SON, that whosoever believeth in Him should not perish, but have everlasting LIFE.

St John 14:18; "I (Jesus), (said) I will not leave you comfortless, I will come to you."

(19) "Yet a little while, and the world sees Me no more; but ye see Me, because I live, ye shall live also. (20) At that day ye shall know that I am in my Father (God), and ye in Me, and I in you."

St John 1:29 says: "John the Baptist saw Jesus coming unto him, and saith, behold the Lamb of God, which taketh away the SINS of the world."

St [Matthew 8:24 "Behold, there arose a great tempest in the sea, insomuch that the ship was covered with the waves; but He (JESUS) WAS ASLEEP. (25) And His disciples (said), awoke Him, saying, Lord, save us. We perish. (26) And He saith unto them, why are you fearful, O ye of little faith? Then Jesus arose, and rebuked the winds and the sea; and there was a great calm. (27) What manner of Man is this, that even the winds and the sea obey Him!"

I thought as I came to the end, of this Book I would tell you what I thought about "LOVE". Like the Old Song says: "What the world needs now is LOVE, SWEET LOVE".

Before I end this book, I would like for you to STOP and read the first few chapters of Genesis in the King James' version. Pay close attention to the word Heaven and when Heavens was first mentioned. Pay close attention to God and then LORD God creating our world as we know it today. Pay close attention to the LORD

God saying to Adam; "in the day you eat of the tree of knowledge, you shall surely die". Then remember in the book of Peter; he, said, "a day in the site of the Lord is as a thousand years, and a thousand years as a day". Adam lived over 600 years then died. Pay close attention to the LORD God walking in the Garden to talking with Adam and Eve. Pay close attention to God saying through Moses, inspired by God, "that our world was VOID and without form". NOTHING was alive on earth—NOTHING. Pay close attention to ALL the things we have talked about in this book. I believe EVERY word in the Bible. I will be writing other books in the future, explaining a lot of things in the Bible.

I hope and pray that this book will cause you to read the Bible more for understanding from God. Pray as you read the Bible, and God will reveal unto you the TRUTH.

I want to end this part of the book the same way the King James' interpretation on the Bible is. Revelation 22:16 to 21.

"I Jesus have sent mine angel to testify unto you these things in the churches, I am the Root

and the Offspring of David, and the bright and morning Star. (17) And the Spirit and the bride say, come. And let him that heareth say, come. And him that is athirst come. And whosoever will, let him take the water of life freely. (18) For I testify unto every man that hearth the words of the prophecy of this book. If any man shall add unto these things, God shall add unto him the plagues that are written in this book. (19) And if any man shall take away from the words of this book of this prophecy, God shall take away his part out of the book of life, and out of the holy city, and from the things which are written in this book. (20) He which testify these things saith, surely, I come quickly. Amen. Even so, come, Lord Jesus Christ be with you all. Amen."

“Circle of Love”

"Circle of Love"

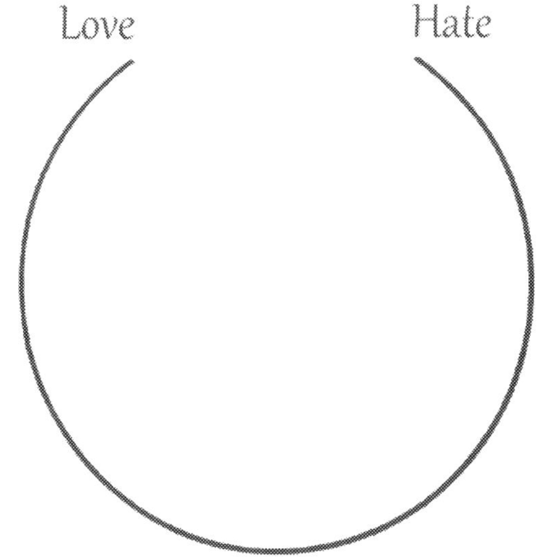

"CIRCLE OF LOVE"

By J. Harvey Hames

LOVE is so strange, unique and unusual. LOVE is so "God like" until I am not sure I can explain it to you or anyone? However, I will try to explain.

LOVE is something I have thought about even while beginning in high school. Looking around seeing couples in love one day and the next day they hated each other. NO, LOVE is NOT like that. Hopefully in this book I will be able to express how I feel about LOVE.

Can you picture a large circle with a small opening at the top? It is not a complete circle. At one end of the opening is LOVE. The other end of the opening is HATE.

Now picture yourself in LOVE or HATE. You cannot be at both ends of the incomplete circle at one time.

Just as an example, you are on the end that says HATE. Sorry to tell you, but you cannot go straight to LOVE. You have to go all the way around the circle to LOVE. Now as an example you are at the

end that says LOVE. You cannot jump across the opening and go straight to HATE. You have to go around the circle to get to HATE. Listen, you cannot jump across the opening from LOVE to HATE. It must be done like this. You cannot jump across the opening from HATE to LOVE. LOVE is a million miles from HATE. HATE is a million miles from LOVE.

Is this beginning to make some sense?

All of my life, I have watched people go from LOVE to HATE in one hour, day or night. Sorry to tell you, but that cannot be done. You need to start thinking about going around the circle to get from LOVE to HATE. That is the ONLY way it can be completed if you are truly in LOVE.

You see a lot of people think they are in LOVE. Therefore, when they fall out of LOVE, they go straight across the opening to HATE. They were NOT in LOVE. I do not care what it is that you feel. Maybe it is sex, desire, lust or just wanting someone. Let me say it again, you were not in LOVE. Trust me you have to go all the way around the circle to get to HATE.

I know that you have watched people all of your life go immediately from LOVE to HATE. Let me emphasize that they were NOT in LOVE.

Let me ask you a question about LOVE. Is it not the most wonderful thing that God has given to us? It can be everlasting. It can be eternal. It can be a feeling that will never leave you until you die. It can also be a feeling that you condition yourself to not LOVE. However, it cannot come overnight. It is something you have to work hard at to get LOVE out of your life. You have to go all the way around the incomplete circle. Yes, you can stop loving someone. Yes, you can get over someone, if you were truly in LOVE. I will say it again you cannot get over someone overnight if you were truly in LOVE. You MUST go around the circle from LOVE to HATE. NOT jump over the vacant opening.

Please understand that LOVE is something that God gives us. So many people play with it. So many people think they were in LOVE. So many people get LOVE and infatuation confused. They get LOVE and desire confused. They mistaking take the idea of LOVE for lust. They do not

understand what LOVE really is. After seeing the opposite sex or the same sex saying "I am in LOVE", I feel they have no idea what LOVE is. LOVE is something that you have to work on and with. A flower cannot blossom without sunshine, and men or women cannot live without LOVE. Without rain nothing grows

So, learn to embrace the storms in your life. I will never say that LOVE is a bed of roses. It is not.

Attraction must to be the first thing.

Then desire or want?

Then working to get what you really want?

Then after a while LOVE starts to come into your life.

Have you seen a man not very nice looking, and he is with a lady very nice looking?

Have you seen a lady not very nice looking, and she is with a man very nice looking?

Looks has very little to do with a relationship. Feelings have a lot to do with a relationship.

After being around someone for a while, you just want or desire to know them better. Some people call it cat and mouse, puppy love or just playing around.

Can you see that you need to go all the way around the incomplete circle?

Your greatest test is when you are able to bless someone else while you are going through your own storm.

I went to a meeting place for young people for many years after I was divorced. I would see many men after just meeting a lady say "I LOVE you". I would just laugh because I knew in a few days they would be separated. People say the word LOVE and do not even know what it means. Many times they are playing a role. Maybe they are just saying what they think the other person wants to hear. Maybe the other person does want to hear that. Maybe they need to hear someone tell them they LOVE them. Trust me that is not the way that LOVE starts.

I dated my wife for approximately three years before we got married. Yes, I was a virgin when

we got married. Did I LOVE her? Yes, I did. I was not completely happy, but I was working on it. Marriage is not a 50/50% thing that couples do. It is a 100/100% thing that they have to do. Jumping ahead for a number of years, we separated. It took me months to get over her. At the time, I also left the church I was the assistant pastor. It DID NOT take a day, or several nights or several days. I am telling you that it took me months to go from LOVE to out of LOVE. I never did want to go to HATE. I stopped somewhere on the circle. Not at HATE. I just fell out of LOVE. LOVE DOES NOT HAVE TO TURN TO HATE.

Remember the circle I have been talking about. LOVE is from God. You do not have to go from LOVE to HATE. You can stop somewhere on the circle. However, you cannot leave and forget true LOVE in a night. It does not work like that.

The same is with HATE. You do not have to HATE someone and go all the way around to circle to find LOVE.

All I am trying to say is that LOVE and HATE are at opposite ends. They are totally different. They are not the same. It is Black and White. It is Day

and Night. They are not close friends. They are not anywhere near each other.

So let me ask again. Why do people LOVE someone one day and the next day they HATE them. It is because they do not understand what LOVE is all about. LOVE is a heavenly experience. LOVE is a feeling that can only come from a heavenly experience. LOVE is something that once you have it you will never want to give it up. You will never want to let it go. You will always want to hold on to it. You will need to nourish it. You will always want it to grow. You will always want it to increase. The experience of having LOVE is like nothing else you will ever experience in life. How can that go to HATE overnight?

Let me go about it in another way. I do not know if you believe in God or not? However, His son Jesus was trying to explain it once and He said there are "gifts of the Spirit" from God. Jesus mentioned nine of the gifts. Guess what the very first one He mentioned was? Yes, it was LOVE. It is a spiritual gift from God.

As a boy I could never understand why God gave His son to die. However, later in life I realized that

"God so LOVED the world that He gave His only begotten Son" (St John 3-16). How can that be? God is a just God. However, He gave His son's life for all of our sins. Not because Jesus was sinful, but because all of us are. I guess I am saying all of this to try and explain what LOVE really is. It is from God. For that reason, do not use it or treat it like one day you are in LOVE and the next day you HATE the same person.

I do not want to be vain. However, I think there were several ladies that could have LOVED me. Maybe if I were willing I could have LOVED them. At that time in my life I was not willing. Many ladies said they would do ANYTHING that would make me happy. Trust me; I did not want to be happy in that way at that time.

After being single and dating a number of ladies. I did not want to get involved with any lady. I had been watching for years how people were using LOVE. I did not want anything to do with it. Every year that passed I felt stronger and more convinced that I did not want anything to do with LOVE. I loved my family and friends but I was NOT in LOVE and I loved it. It was so

simple. It was so easy to live without LOVE. I loved God. Nevertheless, I just could not get into LOVE. I was a million miles from HATE. I did not HATE anyone. I was not in LOVE with anyone. I was down in that valley between LOVE AND HATE. It was wonderful. It was a very simple life of not being in LOVE. I was happy to remain in that stage of my life. Yes, I was attracted to a number of ladies. However, I was not willing to go to that part of the circle. I was fine the way I was at the time. Learning to be single and loving it had gotten easy.

Then…

If you truly want it to lead to LOVE, you need to mean it with your spirit—not just your body.

I was tired. I was getting older. I was ready to change my life to something different. I was ready to start around that circle. Maybe even try again to LOVE. On and off I had started dating a certain wonderful lady. I kept trying to remain single and not get involved. It was refusing to go all the way around that circle again. More than three years had passed and then I asked that lady if I bought a condo would she like living

together? Well, we did. I guess that is when I started around that circle one more time. Well it has taken me years to get around that circle. God has helped me to stop being afraid. He gave me strength to try again. After many years I think I am over that VALLEY. I sure hope so. Yes, there are times when I got frighten. Yes, there are times when I would say; "what are you doing Harvey"? Yes, there have been many times I have thought of walking away.

However, I was just seeing how things are working out. It has been many years at this point. In fact, I have lived with this lady longer than I have lived with anyone in my life including my mother. Sometime without me knowing, I had gone all the way around the circle. I am no longer still going around that circle. I am not still getting close to the finish line. I am at the finish line of LOVE.

Even though it is a little hard for me to say: "is it LOVE"? I do not know how I got all the way around the circle. I have arrived at LOVE. I have!!! I have!!! I have!!!

Now I am more experienced to say that it takes years SOMETIMES to reach that word they call LOVE.

The first time it was easy because I was young and inexperienced. Now I am older and very experienced. I know more than ever what LOVE really is.

Reach back in your life now and try to remember how LOVE started in your life. Maybe it did not take long for you to get around that circle. Not like me taking a long time. Some people can just “do it”. They can get around that circle in a very short time. Nevertheless, remember that if it does not work it will take you some time to go back around that circle. NO you cannot go straight across to HATE or out of LOVE. It does not work like that. You cannot say the next day “I HATE you”. “I have fallen out of LOVE with you”. If you were truly in LOVE you cannot really mean that. You might tell yourself that, but you cannot. Again think back in your life of the person that you LOVED. Remember how it ended. Remember how you felt after it was over. Remember how long it really took you to

get over them? Did you go around the circle fast or slow? I do not know how long it took you to go around the circle. All I know is that it took me a long time to go to LOVE, and a long time to go away from LOVE.

LET ME STOP FOR A MOMENT AND SAY IT DOES NOT HAVE TO GO FROM LOVE TO HATE. YOU CAN STOP HALFWAY AROUND THE CIRCLE AND JUST SAY; "NOW I DO NOT LOVE YOU WITH LOVE LIKE A COUPLE ANYMORE". THAT IS OKAY. THAT IS THE WAY IT SHOULD BE. IF YOU ONCE LOVED SOMEONE IT SHOULD NEVER, NEVER EVER TURN INTO HATE!

That is the reason I came up with the idea of a circle with a small opening at the top. LOVE is on one end and HATE is on the other. I am trying to use a symbol so you can see what I am trying to tell you. It is NOT how you start LOVING or HATING that I am trying to express. It is after being totally in LOVE and then falling totally out of LOVE. That is what I am trying to express how it works. HATE is a million miles from LOVE. LOVE is a million miles from HATE. Let me say it again and again. You cannot go directly from LOVE

to HATE. That is all I am trying to say. This is my philosophy. I have never seen this in a textbook. I have seen it in movies. I have seen some of my friends go from one to the other in one day. How can you do that? Trust me you cannot. Trust me you have to go around the circle. Some go slow and others go faster. Without saying it so many times, you have to go around that circle to go from LOVE to HATE, or out of LOVE. Without repeating myself if you were truly in LOVE, you cannot go in a few hours straight to HATE, or out of LOVE. There is a HUGE missing gap/space between LOVE and HATE.

Maybe you think I am crazy for even writing this book. This is the way I feel. This is the way I believe. This is the way you should believe. This is the way you should think. This is the way it really works.

I have had a lot of friends in my life. I have dated a lot of ladies. No, I have NOT been truly in LOVE with more than just two ladies. I have been afraid of LOVE for many years. Why? Because I know you have to go all the way around that circle. I was not willing to do that. I would get

part of the way around the circle and not go all the way. I would stop after going part of the way around the circle.

Call me a realist, dreamer, softy, believer or any other descriptive word you want to use, but I have studied, watched and experienced with many hours of finding out what LOVE really is.

Trust me—I did not just set down and start writing about this "CIRCLE OF LOVE". I have thought this through for many years.

Sometimes I wonder if some of us are 30 years old, and our mind is 12 or 30 or 50. Believe it or not, that does make a difference. When you are 30 and thinking like a 12 year old, how can you LOVE that special person in your life the right way. When you are 30 and mentally are 50 years old, I feel you have to adapt to LOVING that special person in a certain way. Am I making any since? Mentally you need to be your real age. Mentally you do not have to act your real age. However, mentally you need to approach the subject of LOVE at the age of 30 years old, if you are 30. I hope this additional thought makes since to you? Most of the time that special person is

mentally the age they say they are. If not, then you have a right to act a different age. Sorry, but I needed to cover all aspects of your LOVE life.

It is amazing how five minutes with the wrong person feels like an eternity, yet five hours with the right one seems like just a moment.

Now let us talk about another type of LOVE. Are you ABLE to LOVE people who DO NOT LOVE you? When you realize how much God loves you—with an extravagant, irresistible unconditional LOVE – then His LOVE will change your entire focus on life. If we do not receive God's LOVE for us, we'll have a hard time loving other people. I am talking about loving people who are unlovely, unlovable, difficult, irritable, different, or demanding.

You cannot LOVE that person until you have God's LOVE coming through you. You need to know LOVE so it can overflow out of your life into others.

The tongue has no bones, but it is strong enough to break a heart. So be very careful with all of your words.

All of us can LOVE THOSE WHO love us back. Becoming a master lover means you learn to LOVE the unlovable – when you LOVE people who do not LOVE you.

That is when you can LOVE people who irritate you. That is when you can LOVE people who stab you in the back or gossip about you. This may seem like an impossible task, and it is. That is why we need God's LOVE so we can then LOVE others.

As humans we cannot comprehend how to love someone that hates us. We cannot quite understand how to turn the left cheek when someone slaps us on the right one. When most people would learn how to hate a certain person, you can learn how to LOVE that person.

What is it about human beings that give us the ability to LOVE when we would normally HATE? It is a spiritual part of our being that Jesus had when they were hanging Him on the cross, and He said "Father forgive them for they know not what they do". I DO NOT know how to explain it. I DO NOT even understand it. However, I know that there is something inside of us that is like

God. Something we might not ever be able to put our finger on. I feel it has to be spiritual. It has to be beyond our comprehension. It has to be something we cannot touch, feel or see. Yes, it is something beyond us. It is something Heavenly. Sorry, but I cannot explain what it is that would make us LOVE someone that does not want or needs to be LOVED.

I am getting older in age and I have had a lot of different experiences. I have met a lot of people. Trust me. There are just a few people that will LOVE someone when the other person hates them. I am talking about a LOVE that very few people have. A LOVE that there are just a few people know about it. It is a LOVE that many people do not practice.

Can you understand me? I am trying to tell you about a LOVE that most people DO NOT even know about. Yes, "LOVE your enemy". Yes, "LOVE those who despitefully use you". Yes, I am talking about that person that is unlovable. I am NOT talking about the devil. I am talking about a person that might seem like the devil, but they are human.

It is easy to say LOVE all people. Yes, that would cover it. However, you and I both know that most people do not LOVE everybody. I am saying everyone in life that you meet. Have I made my point?

Another way to describe LOVE is two people having a half circle/half moons put together to make a complete circle. Once they become a circle they become a whole circle. Like marriage you become as one. I am just trying to get you to open your mind as to what the circle of LOVE means.

I believe we have a human and a spiritual part of us. The human is blood, bone, skin, heart, lungs, etc. The spiritual part of us is something you can feel, however, unless you have supernatural vision you cannot see. That is what you LOVE with. Not your bones, blood, skin, heart, lungs, etc. It is the enter part of you that you cannot see.

For all of you that are reading this book and do not believe in a body and a spirit, just try to accept it for now. It will be a lot easier in reading the lines in this book.

I remember in the beginning of Zig Ziglar's book: "See, You At The Top". Zig told a story of John Jones. He lived in New York City. John wanted to go to Boston, so he went to the airport and bought a ticket. Having a few minutes to spare, he walked over to some scales, stepped on them, inserted a coin and down came his fortune: "Your name is John Jones, you weigh 188 pounds and you are going to catch the 2:20 to Boston." John was astounded because all of the info was correct. He figured this must be a trick, so he stepped back on the scales, inserted another coin and down came his fortune: "Your name is still John Jones, you still weigh 188 pounds and you are still going to catch the 2:20 to Boston." Now he was more puzzles than ever. Sensing a trick, he decided to "fool" whoever or whatever was responsible. John went into the men's room and changed clothes. Once again, he stepped on the scales, inserted his coin and down came his fortune: "Your name is still John Jones, you still weigh 188 pounds—but you just missed the 2:20 to Boston."

Why do you feel tricked in life? Accept things in life. You do not understand? Just go with it.

Now back to you believing that you have a Body and a Spirit. You and I see, feel and know that you have a body. That is easy! However, you must realize that you have a Spirit also. This is what I want to cultivate and make you use. This is what I want you to realize that you have. Practice with it. Try it. Know that you do have a Spirit. Like John Jones on his way to Boston—believe it. It does NOT matter if you have NEVER realized in your entire life that you have it. Let me get past the point that you have a Body and a Spirit.

The greatest Teacher that has ever lived on earth was once talking to a very rich man 2000 years ago and said this: "The wind bloweth where it listenth, and thou hearest the sound thereof, but canst not tell whence it cometh, and whither it goeth; so is every one that is born of the Spirit". Nicodemus answered and said unto him. "How can these things be?" Jesus answered and said unto him, "art thou a master of Israel, and knowest not these things?"

St. John chapter 3 versus 8 to 10, I feel that Jesus was trying to say, you cannot see the spirit. However, you can feel the wind blowing, and

you do not know where is comes from or where it goes. He was trying to describe to a rich man that we (humans) have a spirit. We cannot see it, but we can feel it.

Hopefully, we are now past the point of believing that we have a Spirit. Practice with the Spirit until you realize it is there.

Describe Jesus, Jesus, Jesus…

You see—God's LOVE is for everyone. That is what our LOVE should be.

You can touch someone with your hand, body, etc. Notwithstanding the thought, you NEED to LOVE them with your Spirit. Something you cannot see.

However, when you give a gentle smile, tender touch, and full of feeling romantic talk that is something you can see and feel.

JUST REMEMBER YOU CAN DO THESE THINGS AND NOT BE IN LOVE. Never the less, I feel, if you are truly, smiling, tenderly, touching, and have romantic talks that it will lead to LOVE. After so long, the other person can tell if it is real or not.

If it is only Lust or Attraction, the other person will know after a time. I have looked in temples, churches and mosques, but the only place I have found the divine LOVE is within my own heart.

LOVE is not what you say. LOVE is what you do.

Do not believe those who tell you they LOVE you. Believe those who SHOW YOU they LOVE you.

True LOVE comes from the soul. Far beyond the physical chemistry that cannot be explained or understood. It is really simple.

SOMETIMES ALL YOU NEED IS A HUG FROM THE RIGHT PERSON AND ALL YOUR STRESS WILL MELT AWAY.

The best things in life are free; smiles, hugs, a kiss, family, friends, sleep, LOVE, laughter and good memories.

MISSING SOMEONE IS YOUR HEART'S WAY OF REMINDING YOU THAT YOU "LOVE" THEM.

Everything we do, we do for LOVE. The beauty of LOVE is that in giving it away, you leave with more than you had before.

THE “LOVE” WE GIVE AWAY IS THE ONLY “LOVE” WE KEEP.

“LOVE” IS A GAME THAT TWO CAN PLAY AND BOTH CAN WIN.

It is 3 AM and I could not sleep. I am wide awake again.

Maybe I should explain that LOVE leads to a deeper feeling and action between a man and woman. There is a point that both of you get to where you want more. That is when you start experimenting with touching, kissing, rubbing and imaging there is something more that you want to do with this person. Yes a deeper experience in life. You have heard of it all of your life. Now maybe both of you are at the point of experiencing more. You both start getting undressed. You get more excited by seeing the other person nude. Then it happens. Yes, both of you start doing more and more.

After a short time, your two bodies are touching and both of you LOVE and enjoy it very much. Then you get hot and start breathing heavy and “mother nature” takes over and the two of you

become as one. You both get to a point that you cannot stop what you are doing. You both LOVE it. After being catch up in ecstasy you realize that you have taken the final step in LOVE. Your two warm bodies hold each other tight and you continue to kiss. After a while you come back to the real world and realize what both of you have done. You LOVE it. Many times you cannot stop. You want it to last forever. You feel that you are in another world. Now the "ice" has been broken. Both of you know what you have just done. You look at each other and say to yourself what is next. Keep on doing what you just did or talk about living together or should I say getting married? If you are NOT already married.

It is decision time. You have gone completely around the "Circle of LOVE". That is the final act of the play. Now there is a lot of talking. Now there is time to know if both of you feel the same way. You MUST be truthful with each other. You MUST say what is on your mind. DO NOT LIE TO EACH OTHER. This is not the time for that. Just realize that what you just did is the most beautiful and wonderful thing that God has given to the human race.

Let me leave you with a few saying…

People who LOVE you for who you are rather than what you can do for them are the best kind of friend.

NO MATTER HOW BUSY A PERSON IS, IF THEY REALLY CARE, THEY WILL ALWAYS FIND TIME FOR YOU.

I am slowly learning that some people are not good for me, no matter how much I LOVE them.

Perfect people are not real, and real people are not perfect.

EVERYONE IS BEAUTIFUL IN THEIR OWN WAY BECAUSE GOD MAKES NO MISTAKES.

IT IS OKAY TO CRY. EVEN THE SKY CRIES SOMETIMES.

COLLECT MOMENTS NOT THINGS. COLLECTED MOMENTS LAST FOREVER.

One big universe and I have the privilege of meeting and writing to you.

LOVE is the closest thing we have to magic.

A million men can tell a woman she is beautiful, but the only time she will listen is when it is said by the man she LOVES.

Every day is a second chance.

You can always make more money, but you only have a set number of days to make more memories.

LOVE is the reason we are here on earth.

How beautiful it is to find someone who asks for nothing but your company.

Setting silently beside someone who is hurting may be the best gift we can give.

Never ignore someone who LOVES and CARES for you because someday you will realize you have lost a diamond while you were busy collecting stones.

Remember, anyone can LOVE you when the sun is shining. In the storms is where you LEARN who truly cares for you.

AFTER. I wish I could have just one more day with you. I miss you!

A typical LOVE song would go something like this:

Why did you leave me and go away?
Oh, when I longed for you each day
Why did you say God needs you more?
Than, my love could ever afford

Why did you feel your time was done?
And you were willing to finish and run
I wanted you to fight for us
And not be willing to give up and run

Don't you know how much it hurts
To say Goodbye to the one that you love?
Each day now, all I want is to say
Why did you leave me and go away?

Why did you leave and go away?
While all I longed was for you to stay
And all you said is "I must Go".
I knew your time on earth was done

I could not hold you any more with me
God called you home to be with Him
Now all I ask myself each day
Why did you leave and go away?

Printed in the United States
By Bookmasters